PACEMAKER® PRACTICAL ARITHMETIC SERIES

Money
Makes
Sense

Charles H. Kahn
J. Bradley Hanna

GLOBE FEARON

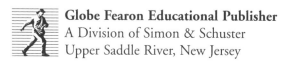
Globe Fearon Educational Publisher
A Division of Simon & Schuster
Upper Saddle River, New Jersey

PACEMAKER® PRACTICAL ARITHMETIC SERIES

Money Makes Sense

Using Dollars and Sense

Working Makes Sense

Buying with Sense

CONTENTS

Director of Editorial and Marketing, Special Education: Diane Galen
Marketing Manager: Susan McLaughlin
Assistant Marketing Manager: Donna Frasco
Executive Editor: Joan Carrafiello
Senior Editor: Stephanie Petron Cahill
Contributing Editor: Jennifer McCarthy
Editorial Assistant: Brian Hawkes
Production Director: Kurt Scherwatzky
Production Editor: John Roberts
Art Supervision: Pat Smythe
Cover Design: A Good Thing Inc.
Interior Design: Thompson Steele Production Services
Electronic Page Production: Thompson Steele Production Services
Illustrators: Thompson Steele Production Services, Teresa Camozzi,
            and Sam Masami Daijogo

Globe Fearon is a trademark of Globe Fearon, Inc.
Pacemaker is a registered trademark of Globe Fearon, Inc.

Printed in the United States of America

    5 6 7 8 9 10   00 99

ISBN 0-8359-3467-5

Does money make sense to you? It should. You will be using money as long as you live. Most people use money almost every day.

You use money when you shop.

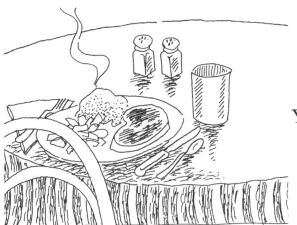

You use money when you eat out.

You use money to pay your bills.

You use money when you travel.

You use money for entertainment.

There are other times when you will use money, too. It makes sense to learn all you can about money.

You may have used money many times. Sometimes it is easy to count money, and other times it seems more difficult. You will be using money all of your life, so it is important to learn about our money system: the history of our money, what the different coins look like, what they are worth, and some hints on how to count money easily and correctly.

While you are learning more about money, you will also be adding to your arithmetic skills. By the time you finish this book, you will have had a lot of practice in adding numbers and "shopping" in different stores. This will help you in school as well as out of school.

This book will help you see how money makes sense. Your teacher will give you all the help you need. You will find that learning about money is not only necessary, but fun, too!

Pretest 1

NAME ______________________________

Draw a line from each word to the coin it names.

dime

dollar

quarter

nickel

penny

half-dollar

one cent

ten cents

one dollar

twenty-five cents

five cents

fifty cents

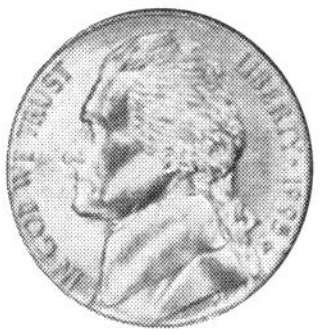

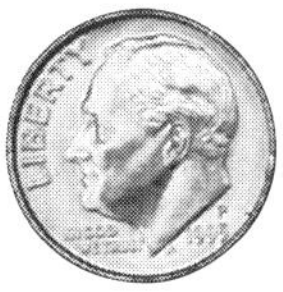

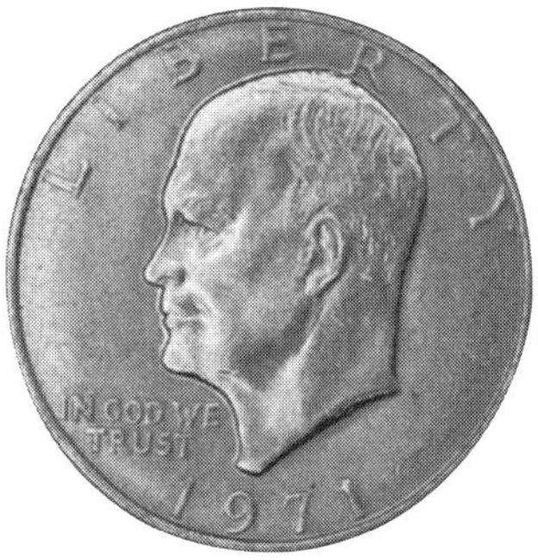

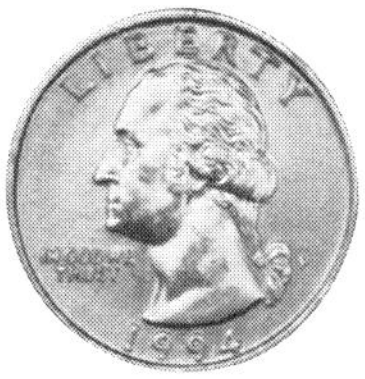

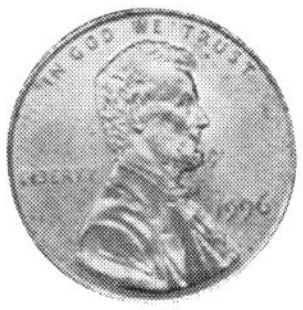

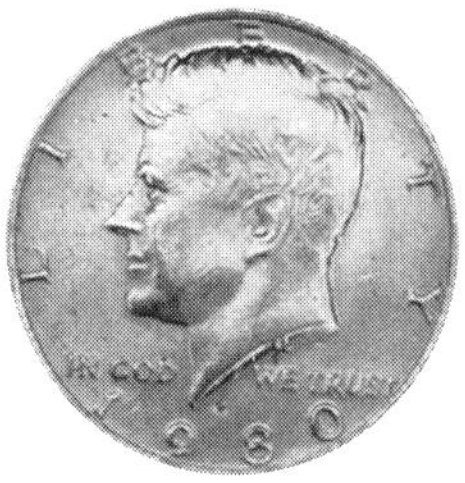

Draw a line from each word to the coin it names.

twenty-five cents

penny

five cents

half-dollar

ten cents

quarter

dime

dollar

fifty cents

nickel

one dollar

one cent

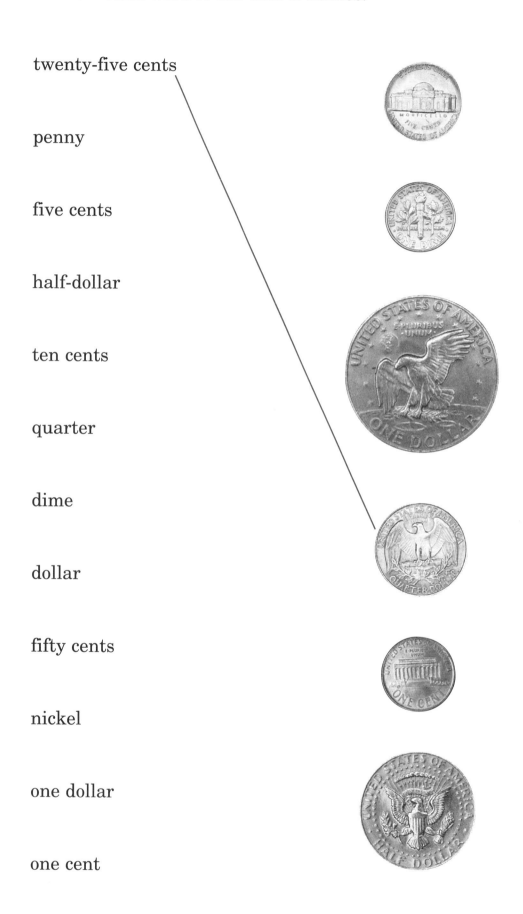

Pretest II

Find the value of each group of coins on the left. Circle the amount on the right that is equal to the value of the coins on the left.

1.  =

5 cents

15 cents

(10 cents)

2.  =

6 cents

11 cents

15 cents

3.  =

30 cents

45 cents

50 cents

4.  =

50 cents

26 cents

35 cents

5.  =

50 cents

75 cents

60 cents

6.  =

80 cents

60 cents

35 cents

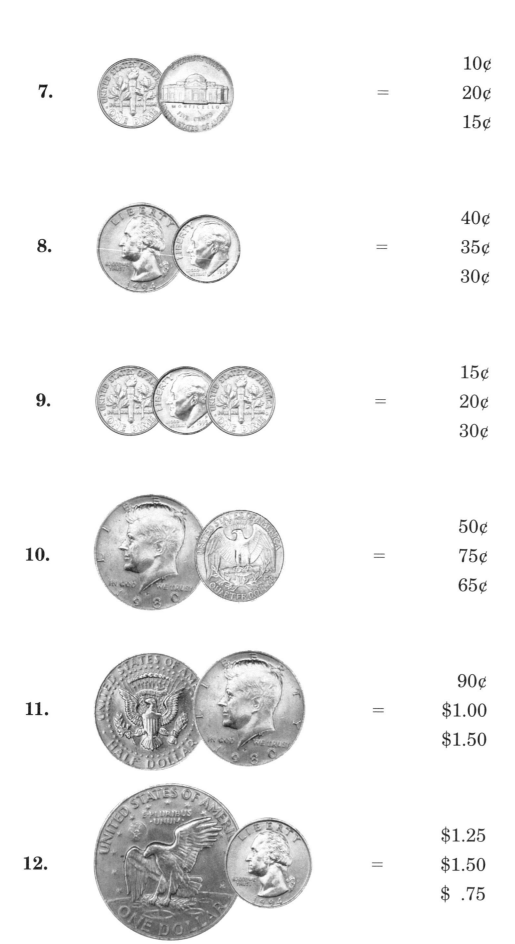

7. $=$ 10¢
20¢
15¢

8. $=$ 40¢
35¢
30¢

9. $=$ 15¢
20¢
30¢

10. $=$ 50¢
75¢
65¢

11. $=$ 90¢
$1.00
$1.50

12. $=$ $1.25
$1.50
$ .75

Most people in our country use money almost every day. But a long, long time ago, people did not use money at all. There were no coins or paper money. When people wanted to get something, they had to trade something else for it.

This is how trading worked.

Brutus was a cabbage farmer. He had more than enough cabbages to feed his family of ten. What they really needed were shoes—and they let Brutus know it!

So Brutus went to see Juno, who was a shoemaker. "I'll trade you 300 cabbages for ten pairs of shoes, Juno," said Brutus. "My cabbages, you know, are the best in town."

"Your cabbages are beautiful," said Juno, "but what am I going to do with 300 of them? Besides, I don't even *like* cabbage. If you had a cow, though, we might make a trade."

So Brutus went to see Marcus. Marcus owned many cows. "Hello there, Marcus!" cried Brutus. "Want to trade a cow for 300 cabbages?"

Marcus looked surprised. "Are you sick or something, Brutus?" he asked. "What would I do with 300 cabbages? I could use pigs, though. Come back with two pigs, and we might make a trade."

Brutus went on to visit Lina, who ran a pig farm. Her pigs were eating her out of house and home. "Am I glad to see you!" cried Lina when she saw Brutus and his cabbages. "How about trading me those cabbages. I'll give you two pigs for them."

"Sold!" cried Brutus. "There are 300 cabbages here. I know your pigs will love them."

Brutus traded his cabbages for two of Lina's pigs. Then he went back to Marcus. He traded the two pigs for one of Marcus' cows. And with his new cow, he went off to see Juno.

Juno was not in his shop when Brutus got there. After a long wait, Juno finally showed up. "Nice cow you have there, Brutus," said Juno. "A present for your wife?"

Brutus was very angry. But he knew he had to be nice to Juno if he wanted shoes for his family. "No," said Brutus, "this cow is not a present for my wife. You told me this morning you would trade shoes for a cow. I have been trading all day to get this cow! Now I want to trade her to you for ten pairs of shoes."

"Let me think about it for a while," said Juno. He thought and thought and thought. Poor Brutus almost fell asleep. But at last Juno said, "All right, the shoes are yours."

Brutus came home with the shoes for his family. Now everyone was happy. Brutus's family had shoes. Juno had his cow. Marcus had his pigs. Lina had cabbages to feed her pigs.

Poor Brutus was very tired from his day of trading. He went straight to bed and fell asleep. Maybe he had a dream. He might have dreamed of the day when people would start using money. If people used money, Brutus could have sold his cabbages for money. Then he could have used the money to buy shoes for his family. This would have saved him a lot of time and work.

Brutus's story is just an idea of what life was like before we had money. People still trade for things they need in some small areas of the world. However, one day, some very wise people really did get together. They had a great idea—using money! They brought all the people of their town together. They told the people that their trading days were over. They said they would teach the people how to use *money*.

The wise people placed six bags of salt on a table. "From now on," they said, "you can give six bags of salt for one cow." Then they took away three of the bags. "For three bags of salt," they said, "you can buy one pig." Then they took away one more bag of salt. "For one bag of salt," they said, "you can buy ten baskets of wheat. Or you can buy one pair of shoes. Or . . ." The wise people went on and on. They named all the things people needed. They named all the things people had been trading.

At first the people just smiled as they listened to the wise people. But they soon caught on. Salt was something that everyone needed. You could always trade it, so you could always use it to get things you needed. *And it was easy to carry around.*

How happy the people were! At last they had *money*. They would not have to spend all their time trading.

Everyone in the town began using salt as money. After a while, the people in the next town began using salt money, too. Soon people all over the country were using salt money. Then people in the next country found out what was going on. They saw how much better it was to use money than to trade. They started using salt money, too.

So it went from country to country. Everyone liked using money. But not everyone thought that salt made the best money. In some countries, people thought it was better to use seashells for money. Others used special balls of clay, special stones, or special pieces of wood.

It was many years after this that people began using metals for money. At first, bars of copper, silver, or gold were used. Then the first metal coin was made. Metal was beaten into a round, flat shape. Then a picture was stamped on one of its sides.

China may have been the first place where coins were made. But the first coins we are sure about came from Lydia—2,600 years ago! Lydia was a country in Asia Minor, where Turkey is today.

Coins were also made in the Greek islands, not far from Lydia. The coins that the Greeks made were very beautiful. They were made of silver. And they had pictures on both sides. Greek coins were used as money in many countries.

As time went on, more and more countries made their own coins. Coins were made in Africa, Asia, and Europe. But the coins of the Romans became the most important. Roman coins were used for hundreds of years in every part of the Roman Empire. And the Roman Empire covered a good part of the world.

Today, every country has its own coins. Paper money has been in use for only a few hundred years. Most countries now have their own paper money, too. Making paper money was another step taken so that money would be easier to carry and use.

In America's early days, people used English, French, and Spanish coins as money. It was not until 1793 that the first United States coins were made.

English

Spanish

French

Coins were made in a place called a mint. The first United States mint was in Philadelphia. This mint turned out gold coins (eagles), silver coins (dollars), and copper coins (cents). Other coins—half-eagles, half-dollars, and so on—were also made there. The gold eagle was worth the most—ten dollars.

Gold Eagle

Half-Eagle

Silver Dollar

Cent

Today there are two mints that make United States coins. These mints are in Philadelphia and Denver. All of our money is in dollars and cents now. The metals used in our coins are copper, tin, zinc, and nickel. Sometimes, gold and silver coins are made to honor a special person or a special event. This coin usually shows a picture of this person or event. People who like to collect coins usually buy them to keep in their coin collection. We call these special gold or silver coins "commemorative coins."

These special coins are made in Philadelphia, Denver, and two other mints located in San Francisco, California, and West Point, New York, that only make special coins. The headquarters for the United States Mint is in Washington, D.C. This is where all decisions are made about making or changing coins.

United States coins have changed over the years. At one time, we had a picture of an American Indian on the penny. And we once had a nickel with a buffalo pictured on it. "Indian head pennies" and "buffalo nickels" are hard to find today. Not long ago, Benjamin Franklin was pictured on the half-dollar. You can still find some of these coins around.

Today the front sides (heads) of all our coins carry pictures of famous Americans. The back sides (tails) show other famous places and things.

Abraham Lincoln is on the penny (one cent).

The back shows the Lincoln Memorial, a building in Washington, D.C.

Thomas Jefferson is on the nickel (five cents).

The back shows Monticello, Jefferson's home in Virginia.

Franklin D. Roosevelt is on the dime (ten cents).

The back shows the torch of freedom with laurel and oak leaves.

George Washington is on the quarter (twenty-five cents).

The back shows the American bald eagle.

John F. Kennedy is on the half-dollar (fifty cents).

The back shows the seal of our presidents.

Dwight D. Eisenhower is on the dollar (one dollar).

The back shows the American bald eagle landing on the moon.

The penny and the nickel have smooth edges. All of the other coins have rough edges. They have many lines cut into them. Many blind people can tell one coin from another by touch. Can you?

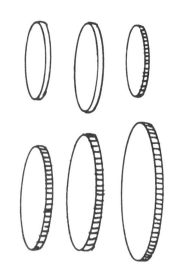

A dollar coin, with Susan B. Anthony on its front, first came out in 1978. Susan B. Anthony helped organize the group that got women the right to vote. Many people collect this coin. Others find they mistake it for a quarter, so they try to avoid using it. For these reasons, you do not see many of these dollars being used today.

A dollar coin with Dwight D. Eisenhower on its front was produced from 1971 to 1978. Eisenhower was the 34th United States president. People collect these coins, too, but you still see them being used from time to time.

United States Bills

Our paper money has looked the same since 1929. In 1996, the Bureau of Engraving and Printing in Washington issued a new $100 bill. There are plans to redesign the fifty-, twenty-, ten-, and five- dollar bills before the year 2000. The new bills will be the same size and color. They will have the same pictures on them, but they will be larger and off-center. There will be special inks in the paper so that people cannot copy the bills.

George Washington's picture is on the front of the dollar bill (one dollar). The back shows the Great Seal of the United States.

All of our paper money is printed in black and green. It is bigger in size than the bill shown here. Our laws say that only the government can print pictures of our money in green. Only the government can print pictures of bills that are the same size as the real bills. Can you guess why we have such laws?

Name the Coins

Write the name and value of each coin in the blank next to it.

1.

_____ quarter _____ twenty-five cents _____

2.

_____

3.

_____

4.

_____

5.

_____

6.

_____

7.

_____

8.

_____

9.

_____

10.

_____

11.

_____

12.

_____

Name the Money

Draw lines from each word to the money it names. All the money must be named.

dime

penny

quarter

dollar

nickel

half-dollar

Write the name of each coin in the blank below it.

1.

dollar

2.

3.

4.

5.

6.

7.

8.

9.

10.

11.

12.

Name the Money

Write the name of each coin or bill in the blank below it.

1.

half-dollar   _____   _____   _____

2.

_____   _____   _____   _____

3.

_____   _____   _____   _____

4.

_____   _____   _____

5.

_____   _____   _____   _____

6.

7.

8.

9.

10.

Name the Coins and Match the Circles

Draw a line from each coin to its name. Then draw another line from the coin to a circle the same size as the coin. If you cannot tell which circles match which coins, place real coins on the circles.

Names	Coins	Circles
dime		
quarter		
penny		
half-dollar		
dollar		
nickel		

Each of these circles is the same size as a United States coin. Under each circle, write the name of the coin it matches. Place real coins in the circles if you are not sure.

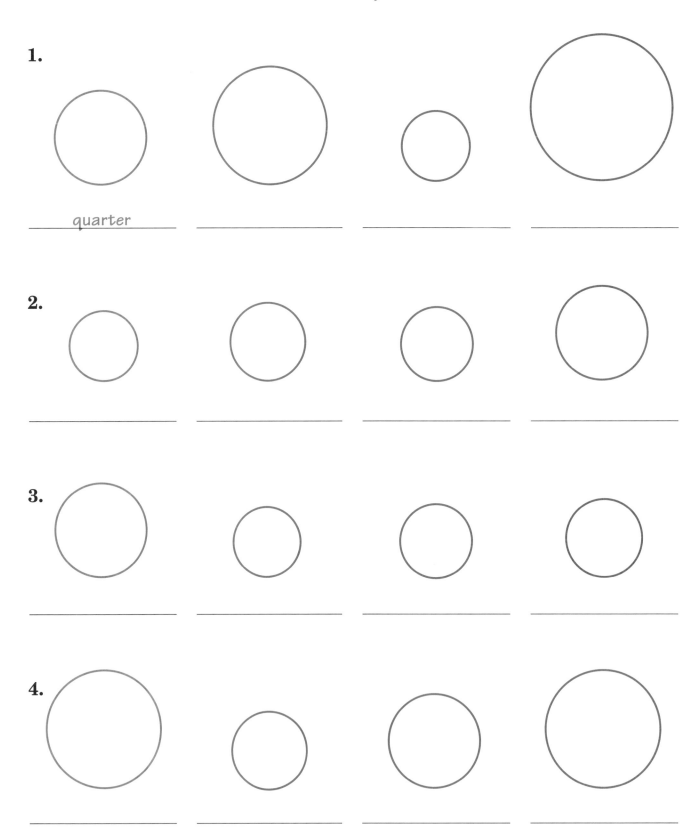

1.

_____quarter_____

2.

3.

4.

Name the Money

The name of a coin or bill tells you how much it is worth—its value. The name or value of money can also be written in numbers. The names or values of United States money are given here in numbers. In the blank under each coin or bill, write its value in words.

$ .01 *or* 1¢ $ .05 *or* 5¢ $ .10 *or* 10¢

____one cent____   _____   _____

$ .25 *or* 25¢ $ .50 *or* 50¢ $1.00 *or* $1

_____   _____   _____

$ 1.00 *or* $1

_____

When numbers are used to name money, signs are used with them. The sign for dollars is **$**. The sign for cents is **¢**. *But these two signs are never used at the same time.* When the dollar sign is used, a decimal point is placed before the numbers for cents.

In the blank under each coin or bill, write its value in numbers. Use the dollar sign and a decimal point.

1.

$ .25 _____ _____ _____ _____

2.

_____ _____ _____ _____ _____

3.

_____ _____ _____ _____

4.

_____ _____ _____ _____ _____

Name the Money

In the blank under each coin or bill, write its value in numbers. Use the cent sign for amounts under a dollar. Use the dollar sign for amounts equal to a dollar.

1.

10¢ _____ _____ _____ _____

2.

_____ _____ _____ _____ _____

3.

_____ _____ _____ _____ _____

4.

_____ _____ _____

Draw a line from each word or value to the coin it names.

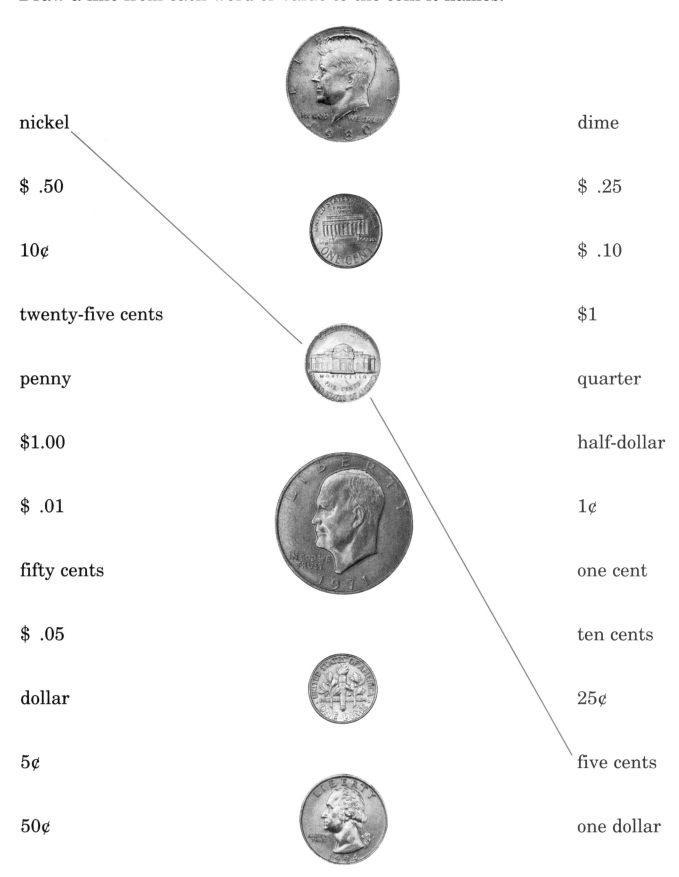

nickel	dime
$ .50	$ .25
10¢	$ .10
twenty-five cents	$1
penny	quarter
$1.00	half-dollar
$ .01	1¢
fifty cents	one cent
$ .05	ten cents
dollar	25¢
5¢	five cents
50¢	one dollar

Counting Money

You may often have more than one coin in your pocket. Then you will want to know how much money you have altogether. To find out, you add up the value of all of the coins. This is called *counting money*.

Counting money is the same as adding numbers. The total value you get is called the *sum*.

$$
\begin{array}{rl}
5 & \text{five} \\
1 & \text{six} \\
1 & \text{seven} \\
+1 & \text{eight} \\
\hline
8 & \textbf{The sum is eight.}
\end{array}
$$

5¢   +   1¢   +   1¢   +   1¢   =   8¢

five   six   seven   eight

The sum is eight cents.

Here are some more examples. Say the words as you count from left to right. Coins of higher value are counted first.

five   six   seven   eight   nine   ten

The sum is ten cents.

ten   fifteen   sixteen   seventeen   eighteen

The sum is eighteen cents.

Count each of these groups of coins from left to right. As you count, say the words and write them in the blanks under the coins. Then write the sum in words.

1.

one   two   three   four   five

The sum is _____ five cents _____

2.

_____ _____ _____ _____ _____ _____ _____

The sum is _____

3.

_____ _____ _____

The sum is _____

4.

_____ _____ _____ _____

The sum is _____

5.

_____ _____ _____

The sum is _____

6.

_____ _____ _____ _____

The sum is _____

How Much Is It?

Count each of these groups of coins from left to right.
As you count, say the words and write them in the
blanks. Write the sum in words under the last coin.

1.

___ten___   ___eleven___   ___twelve___   ___thirteen___   __fourteen cents__
                                                              sum

2.

_____   _____   _____   _____   _____
                                                   sum

3.

_____   _____   _____   _____   _____
                                                   sum

4.

_____   _____   _____   _____   _____
                                                   sum

5.

_____   _____   _____   _____   _____
                                                   sum

6.

_____   _____   _____   _____   _____
                                                   sum

7.

_____ _____ _____ _____ _____
sum

8.

_____ _____ _____ _____ _____
sum

9.

_____ _____ _____ _____ _____
sum

10.

_____ _____ _____ _____ _____
sum

11.

_____ _____ _____ _____ _____
sum

12.

_____ _____ _____ _____ _____ _____
sum

How Much Is It?

Count each group of coins from left to right. As you count, say the words, *but write the amounts in numbers.* Write the sum, using the cent sign, under the last coin in each group.

1.

    _____ 10 _____   _____ 15¢ _____

2.

    _____   _____   _____   _____

3.

    _____   _____   _____

4.

    _____   _____   _____   _____   _____

5.

    _____   _____   _____   _____   _____

6.

    _____   _____   _____   _____   _____

7.

_____

8.

_____

9.

_____

10.

_____

11.

_____

12.

_____

NAME _____

Count each group of coins from left to right. As you count, say the words. Then write the amounts in numbers. Write the sum, using the cent sign, under the last coin in each group.

1. ____50¢____   ____75¢____

2. _____ _____ _____ _____ _____

3. _____ _____ _____ _____

4. _____ _____ _____ _____ _____ _____

5. _____ _____ _____ _____

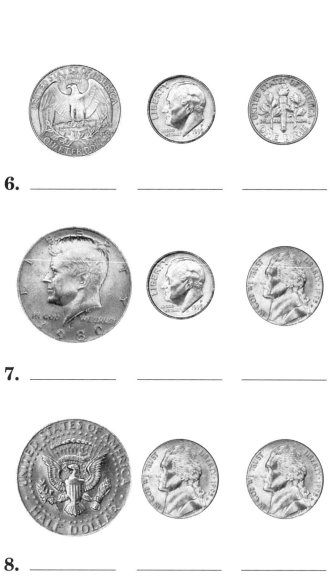

6. _____ _____ _____ _____ _____

7. _____ _____ _____ _____ _____

8. _____ _____ _____ _____ _____ _____

9. _____ _____ _____ _____ _____

10. _____ _____ _____ _____ _____ _____

How Much Is It?

When coins are counted, their sum can be written in three ways. Count each of these groups of coins and write each sum three different ways.

1.   4 pennies

$.04   4¢   four cents

2.   2 nickels

_____   _____   _____

3.   2 dimes

_____   _____   _____

4.   2 quarters

_____   _____   _____

5.   2 pennies

_____   _____   _____

6.   3 dimes

_____   _____   _____

7.   3 pennies

_____   _____   _____

8.   3 nickels

_____   _____   _____

9. 4 dimes

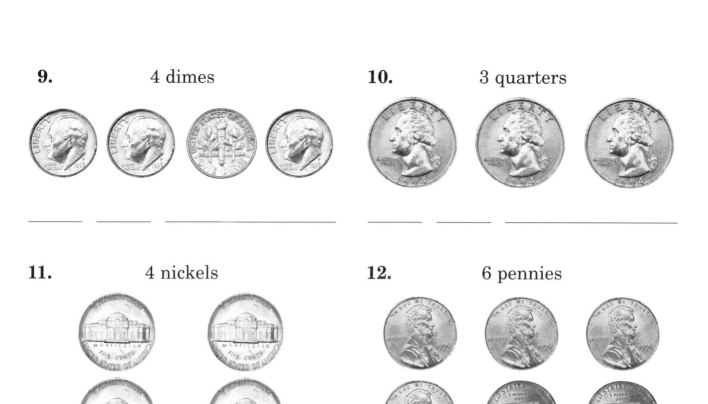

10. 3 quarters

_____ _____ _____

11. 4 nickels

12. 6 pennies

_____ _____ _____

13. 6 nickels

14. 10 dimes

_____ _____ _____

15. 5 dimes

16. 2 half-dollars

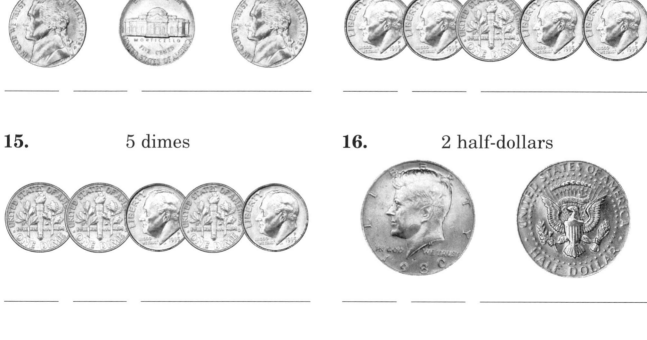

_____ _____ _____

NAME _____

Count each group of coins. Write each sum in three different ways.

1.

$ .10   10¢   _____ ten cents

2.

_____ _____ _____

3.

_____ _____ _____

4.

_____ _____

5.

_____ _____ _____

6.

_____ _____ _____

7.

_____ _____ _____

8.

_____ _____ _____

Count each group of coins. Write each sum using the
cent sign.

9.

_____10¢_____

10.

_____

11.

_____

12.

_____

13.

_____

14.

_____

15.

_____

NAME _____

Fill in the chart below. Start with the first coin in the top row. Add each coin in the left-hand column to this coin, one at a time, recording your answers each time in the box where the two coins you are adding meet. Repeat these steps for each coin in the top row until the chart is filled in.

+					
	2¢				

		15¢			

Fill in the chart below. Start with the first amount of money in the top row. Add each amount in the left-hand column to this amount, one at a time, recording your answers each time in the box where the two amounts you are adding meet. Repeat these steps for each amount in the top row until the chart is filled in.

+	1¢	2¢	3¢	4¢	5¢	6¢	7¢	8¢	9¢	10¢
1¢										
2¢										
3¢				7¢						
4¢										
5¢								13¢		
6¢										
7¢										
8¢										
9¢										
10¢										

How Much Is It?

Find the value of each group of coins. Write each sum
using the dollar sign and a decimal point.

1.

$$\underline{\qquad \$.06 \qquad}$$

2.

_____

3.

_____

4.

_____

5.

_____

6.

_____

7.

_____

8.

_____

9.

_____

10.

_____

11.

_____

12.

_____

13.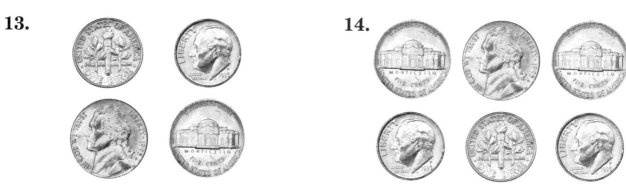

_____

14.

_____

15.

_____

16.

_____

How Much Is It?

How many of each coin are shown? How much are they
worth? Write your answers using the cent sign for totals
less than one dollar in the blanks under the coins.

1.

___ten pennies___   ___10¢___

2.

_____   _____

3.

_____   _____

4.

_____

5.

_____

6.

_____

7.

_____

8.

_____

9.

_____

10.

_____

11.

_____

12.

_____

13.

_____

14.

_____

15.

_____

16.

_____

Name the Coins

Sometimes one coin has the same value as two or more other coins. In these exercises, the coins on the left are worth the same amount of money as the coin on the right. Write the name of the coin on the right in the blank.

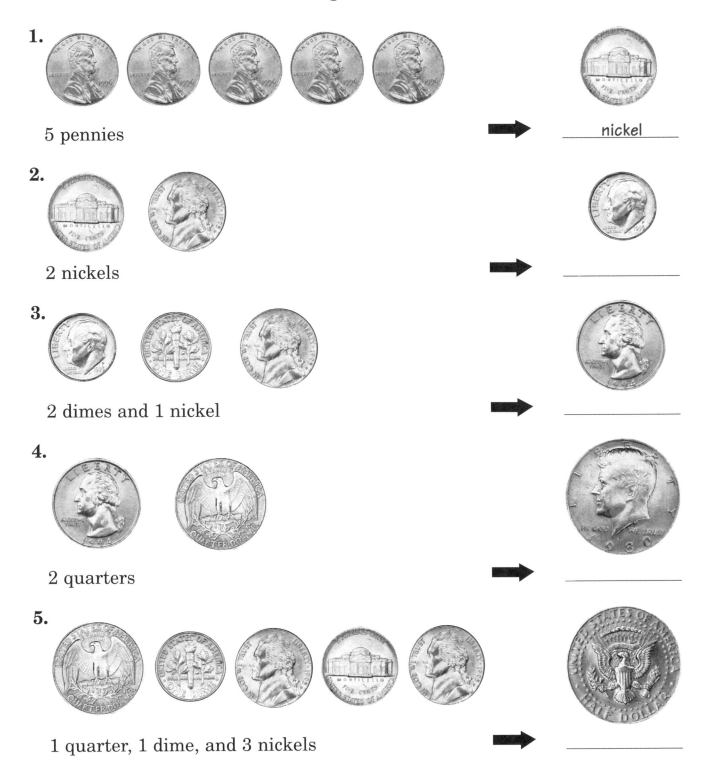

1.

5 pennies ➡ nickel

2.

2 nickels ➡ _____

3.

2 dimes and 1 nickel ➡ _____

4.

2 quarters ➡ _____

5.

1 quarter, 1 dime, and 3 nickels ➡ _____

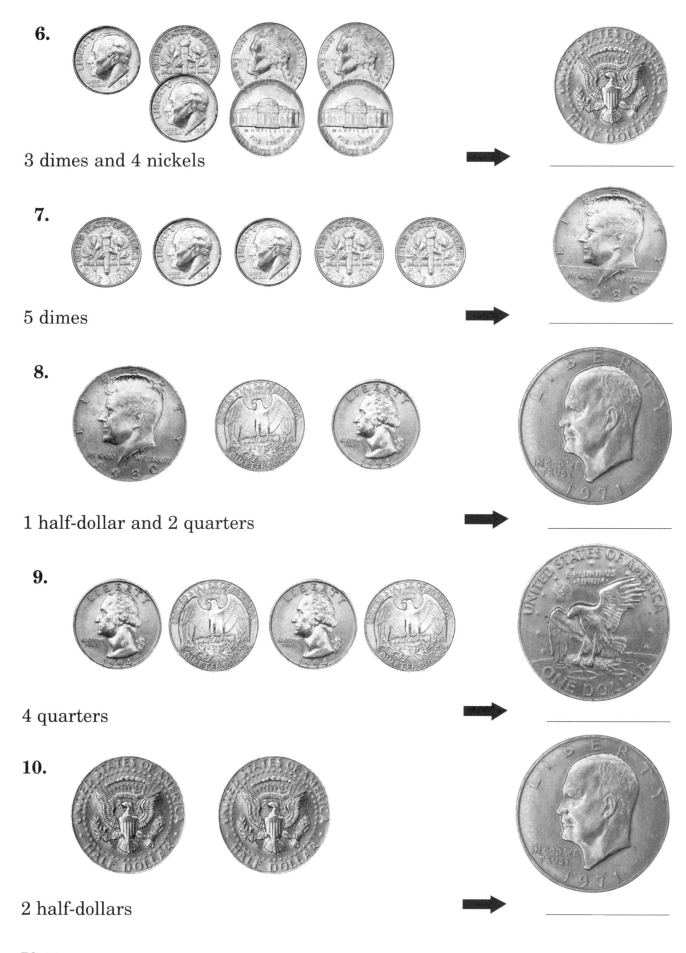

6.

3 dimes and 4 nickels ➡ _____

7.

5 dimes ➡ _____

8.

1 half-dollar and 2 quarters ➡ _____

9.

4 quarters ➡ _____

10.

2 half-dollars ➡ _____

Adding Money

A dollar bill is worth the same as the Eisenhower dollar.
Make X's on the blanks under the coins that add up to
one dollar.

1  is worth:

1.

   X   X   X

2.

3.

4.

Make X's on the blanks under the coins that add up
to the coin on the right.

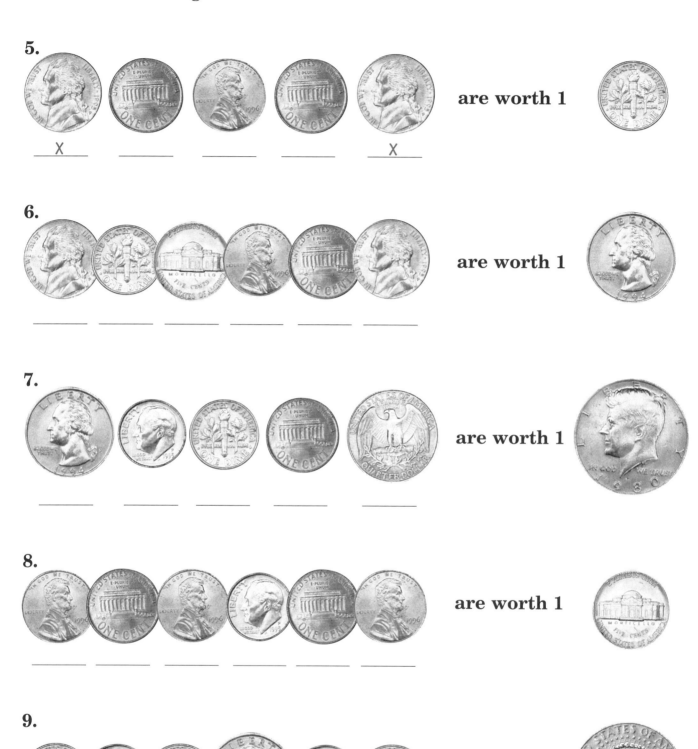

5.

_____ X _____   _____   _____   _____   _____ X _____   **are worth 1**

6.

are worth 1

7.

are worth 1

8.

are worth 1

9.

are worth 1

NAME _____

When the coins on the left are counted, they will equal a single coin. Write the name of the coin in the blank on the right.

1.

dime

2.

_____

3.

_____

4.

_____

5.

_____

6.

_____

7.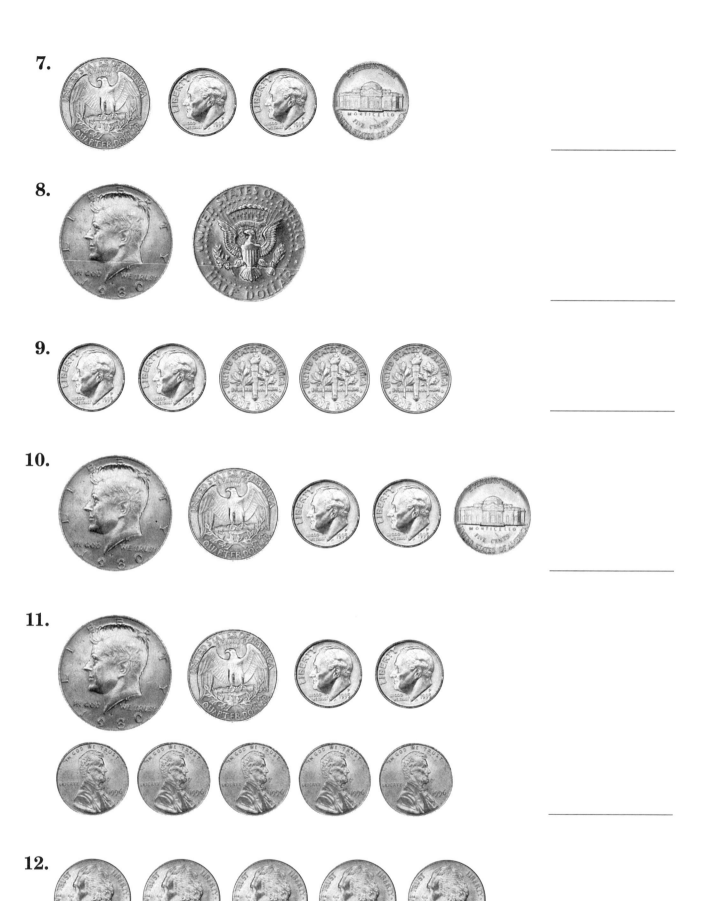

_____

8.

_____

9.

_____

10.

_____

11.

_____

12.

_____

Matching Money

Make X's in the blanks under the amounts of money that match in each row.

1. three cents $1.00   one dollar   50¢

_____   __X__   _____   __X__   _____   _____

2. 75¢   fifty cents   43¢   50¢   penny   half-dollar

_____   _____   _____   _____   _____   _____

3.   nickel   forty cents $ .50   37¢   5¢

_____   _____   _____   _____   _____

4. 30¢   25¢   nineteen cents   quarter   forty-two cents $ .05

_____   _____   _____   _____   _____   _____

5. 13¢   dime $ .25   11¢   quarter   cent

_____   _____   _____   _____   _____   _____

6. 19¢   penny   seventy-five cents   cent $ .01

_____   _____   _____   _____   _____

7. quarter   37¢   16¢ $ .30   thirty-seven cents

_____   _____   _____   _____   _____

8.    14¢   25¢   twenty-five cents $ .05   quarter

____   ____   ____   ____

9. nickel   11¢   eleven cents $ .19   dime

____   ____   ____   ____

10. $ .25      56¢   fifty cents   nickel $1

____   ____   ____   ____

11. dime   13¢ $ .05   23¢   nickel   quarter

____   ____   ____   ____

12. 64¢   sixty-four cents   nickel $ .10

____   ____   ____   ____

13. one dollar   50¢ $1.00 $ .01 $1

____   ____   ____   ____

14. 10¢   twelve cents    $ .15   dime   13¢   penny

____   ____   ____   ____

Matching Money

Make X's in the blanks under the amounts of money that match in each row.

1.  half-dollar   20¢   quarter $ .30   twenty-five cents

___X___   _____   _____   ___X___   _____   ___X___

2. quarter $ .37   87¢   thirty-seven cents $ .56

_____   _____   _____   _____   _____   _____

3. $ .10   one dollar   50¢   ninety cents   100¢   46¢ $1.00

_____   _____   _____   _____   _____   _____   _____

4. 34¢      seventeen cents $ .60   quarter   35¢

_____   _____   _____   _____   _____   _____

5. dime $ .64   75¢   eighty-three cents $ .14   83¢

_____   _____   _____   _____   _____   _____

6. $ .80   sixty cents $ .50   quarter      49¢   half-dollar

_____   _____   _____   _____   _____   _____

7. twenty cents $ .25   20¢   30¢   fifteen cents

_____   _____   _____   _____   _____

8. 75¢   nickel $ .70   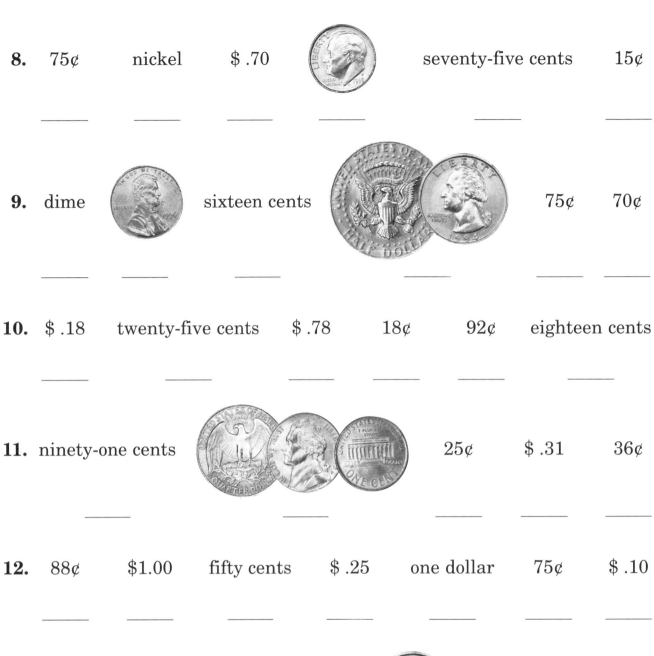   seventy-five cents   15¢

_____   _____   _____   _____   _____   _____

9. dime   sixteen cents   75¢   70¢

_____   _____   _____   _____

10. $ .18   twenty-five cents $ .78   18¢   92¢   eighteen cents

_____   _____   _____   _____   _____   _____

11. ninety-one cents   25¢ $ .31   36¢

_____   _____   _____

12. 88¢ $1.00   fifty cents $ .25   one dollar   75¢ $ .10

_____   _____   _____   _____   _____   _____   _____

13. nickel   cent $ .45   55¢      forty-five cents

_____   _____   _____   _____   _____   _____

14. 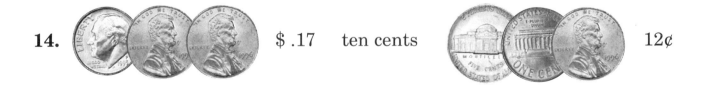 $ .17   ten cents   12¢

_____   _____   _____   _____

What Are They Worth?

Write the total value of the coins in the blanks. Use
numbers and the cent sign.

1.

are worth

<u>   10¢   </u>

2.

are worth

_____

3.

are worth

_____

4.

are worth

_____

5.

are worth

_____

6.

are worth

_____

7.

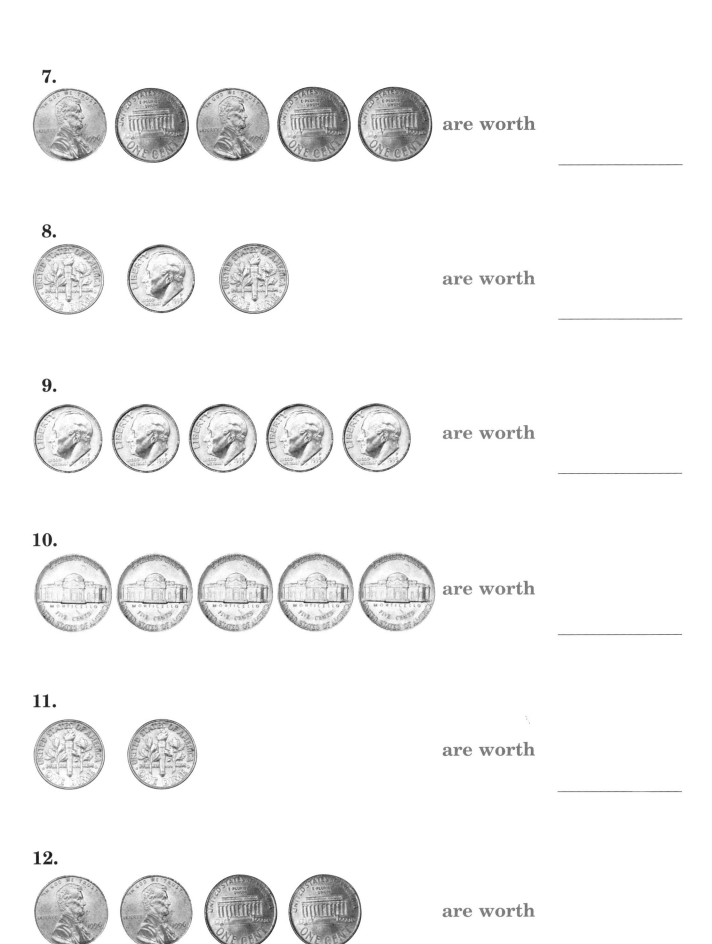

are worth

_____

8.

are worth

_____

9.

are worth

_____

10.

are worth

_____

11.

are worth

_____

12.

are worth

_____

NAME _____

Write the total value of the coins in three different ways.

1.

<u>$ .75</u> <u>75¢</u> <u>seventy-five cents</u>

2.

_____ _____ _____

3.

_____ _____ _____

4.

_____ _____ _____

5.

_____ _____ _____

6.

_____ _____ _____

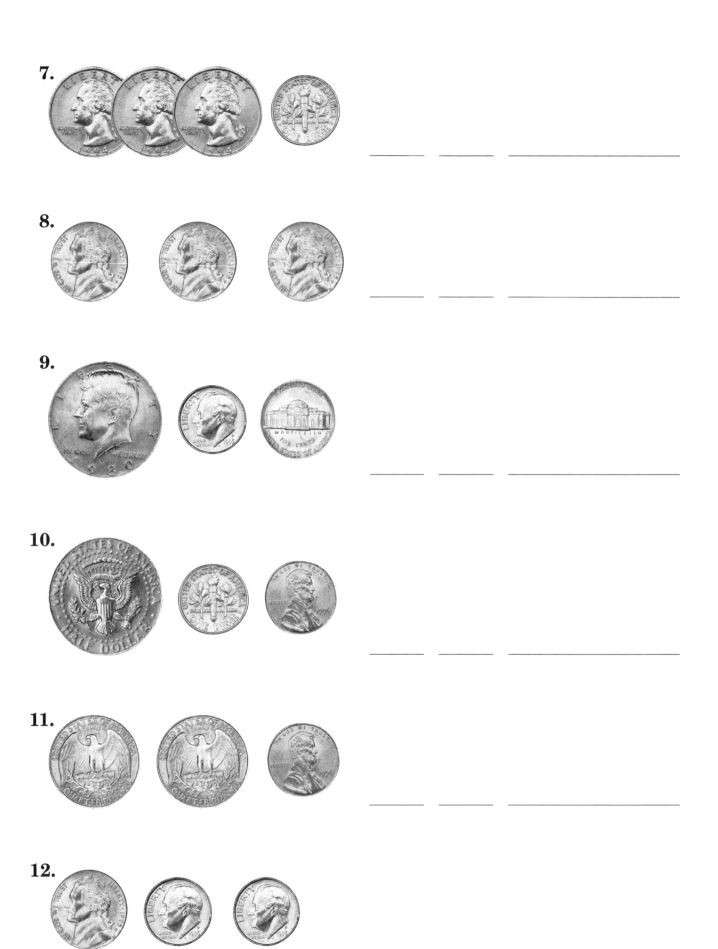

7.

_____ _____ _____

8.

_____ _____ _____

9.

_____ _____ _____

10.

_____ _____ _____

11.

_____ _____ _____

12.

_____ _____ _____

Matching Money

Draw lines connecting the amounts that are the same.

1. thirty cents   25¢ $ .41
     forty-one cents   30¢ $ .25
     twenty-five cents   41¢ $ .30

2. twenty-one cents   15¢ $ .21
     fifteen cents   21¢ $ .27
     twenty-seven cents   27¢ $ .15

3. forty-five cents   60¢ $ .30
     sixty cents   52¢ $ .52
     fifty-two cents   30¢ $ .45
     thirty cents   45¢ $ .60

4. ninety cents   24¢ $ .90
     fourteen cents   90¢ $ .24
     twenty-four cents   14¢ $ .17
     seventeen cents   17¢ $ .14

5. fifteen cents   71¢ $ .15
     ninety-eight cents   11¢ $ .98
     eleven cents   98¢ $ .11
     seventy-one cents   15¢ $ .71

6. thirty-four cents   34¢ $ .65
     eighty-two cents   82¢ $ .19
     sixty-five cents   19¢ $ .82
     nineteen cents   65¢ $ .34

7.	seven cents	6¢	$ .11
	six cents	11¢	$ .06
	eleven cents	13¢	$ .07
	thirteen cents	7¢	$ .13
8.	twenty-one cents	51¢	$ .15
	fifteen cents	21¢	$ .27
	twenty-seven cents	27¢	$ .51
	fifty-one cents	15¢	$ .21
9.	fifteen cents	40¢	$ .15
	thirty cents	60¢	$ .30
	forty cents	30¢	$ .40
	sixty cents	15¢	$ .60
10.	seventeen cents	15¢	$ .17
	eleven cents	98¢	$ .11
	ninety-eight cents	11¢	$ .98
	fifteen cents	17¢	$ .15
11.	nineteen cents	65¢	$ .34
	sixty-five cents	19¢	$ .82
	eighty-two cents	82¢	$ .19
	thirty-four cents	34¢	$ .65
12.	twenty-seven cents	27¢	$ .21
	fifteen cents	31¢	$ .27
	twenty-one cents	15¢	$ .31
	thirty-one cents	21¢	$ .15

How Much Is It?

Find the sum of each group of coins. You may use coins to help find the answer.

You read: 1 dime, 1 nickel, and 3 pennies

You think:

You count: 10 15 16 17 18¢

1. 1 dime, 1 nickel, and 2 pennies   =   _17_ ¢

2. 1 dime, 1 nickel, and 1 penny   =   _____ ¢

3. 1 dime, 1 nickel, and 6 pennies   =   _____ ¢

4. 1 dime and 3 pennies   =   _____ ¢

5. 2 dimes and 1 penny   =   _____ ¢

6. 2 nickels and 3 pennies   =   _____ ¢

7. 1 dime and 3 nickels   =   _____ ¢

8. 1 nickel and 4 pennies   =   _____ ¢

9. 2 dimes and 2 pennies   =   _____ ¢

10. 1 dime, 1 nickel, and 4 pennies   =   _____ ¢

11. 1 dime, 2 nickels, and 2 pennies   =   _____ ¢

12. 1 dime and 4 pennies   =   _____ ¢

13. 1 dime and 7 pennies   =   _____ ¢

14. 3 nickels and 3 pennies   =   _____ ¢

15. 1 dime, 1 nickel, and 8 pennies   =   _____ ¢

Find the sum of each group of coins.

You read: 1 dime,   2 nickels,   and   10 pennies

You think:

You count: 10   20 $.30

16.	1 dime, 2 nickels, and 3 pennies	=		$____.23____
17.	4 nickels and 1 penny	=		$___.___
18.	2 dimes and 3 pennies	=		$___.___
19.	1 dime, 1 nickel, and 6 pennies	=		$___.___
20.	1 dime and 9 pennies	=		$___.___
21.	23 pennies	=		$___.___
22.	2 dimes and 2 pennies	=		$___.___
23.	4 nickels	=		$___.___
24.	1 dime, 1 nickel, and 9 pennies	=		$___.___
25.	1 dime and 2 nickels	=		$___.___
26.	2 dimes	=		$___.___
27.	1 dime and 13 pennies	=		$___.___
28.	3 dimes, 2 nickels, and 4 pennies	=		$___.___
29.	3 nickels and 12 pennies	=		$___.___
30.	5 dimes and 5 nickels	=		$___.___

How Much Is It?

Find the sum of each group of coins.

You read: 1 quarter,   2 dimes,   2 nickels,   and   1 penny

You think:

You count: 25   45   55   56¢

1. 1 quarter, 2 dimes, and 1 penny   =   __46__ ¢

2. 1 quarter, 1 dime, 1 nickel, and 3 pennies   =   _____ ¢

3. 1 quarter and 3 pennies   =   _____ ¢

4. 1 quarter, 1 nickel, and 1 penny   =   _____ ¢

5. 1 quarter, 1 dime, 1 nickel, and 1 penny   =   _____ ¢

6. 1 quarter, 2 dimes, and 4 pennies   =   _____ ¢

7. 1 quarter and 1 penny   =   _____ ¢

8. 1 quarter and 1 nickel   =   _____ ¢

9. 1 quarter and 1 dime   =   _____ ¢

10. 3 quarters and 2 nickels   =   _____ ¢

11. 2 quarters, 3 dimes, and 2 nickels   =   _____ ¢

12. 1 quarter, 4 dimes, and 2 nickels   =   _____ ¢

13. 3 quarters and 17 pennies   =   _____ ¢

14. 2 quarters and six nickels   =   _____ ¢

15. 1 quarter, 4 nickels, and 29 pennies   =   _____ ¢

Find the sum of each group of coins.

You read:	1 half-dollar,	1 quarter,	1 dime,	1 nickel, and 1 penny
You think:				
You count:	50	75	85	90 $ .91

16. 1 half-dollar, 1 quarter, 2 dimes, and 3 pennies = $ *.98*

17. 1 half-dollar, 2 dimes, and 3 pennies = $.___

18. 1 half-dollar, 1 nickel, and 2 pennies = $.___

19. 1 quarter, 4 dimes, and 2 pennies = $.___

20. 1 half-dollar and 25 pennies = $.___

21. 1 half-dollar, 1 quarter, 1 dime, and 3 pennies = $.___

22. 1 half-dollar, 1 nickel, and 1 penny = $.___

23. 1 half-dollar, 1 quarter, 1 dime, and 2 nickels = $.___

24. 3 quarters and 3 nickels = $.___

25. 1 half-dollar, 1 quarter, 2 dimes, and 2 pennies = $.___

26. 1 half-dollar, 1 nickel, and 4 pennies = $.___

27. 1 half-dollar, 3 nickels, and 2 pennies = $.___

28. 1 half-dollar, 3 dimes, and 2 nickels = $.___

29. 1 half-dollar, 4 dimes, and 4 pennies = $.___

30. 1 half-dollar and 2 quarters = $.___

NAME _____

Whenever you add money and use decimal points, you must line up the decimal points. All the money to the left of a decimal point is dollars. The money to the right of a decimal point is cents. Every 100 cents makes one dollar. There must always be two numbers on the cents side of a decimal point.

<table>
<tr><td>$1.00</td><td>+</td><td>$.25</td><td>+</td><td>$.10</td><td>=</td><td>$1.35</td></tr>
<tr><td>one dollar</td><td></td><td>one dollar and
twenty-five cents</td><td></td><td>one dollar and
thirty-five cents</td><td></td><td></td></tr>
</table>

```
  $1.00
   .25
+  .10
------
  $1.35
```

Here are some more examples. Say the words as you count from left to right. Coins and bills of higher value are counted first.

<table>
<tr><td>$1.00</td><td>+</td><td>$1.00</td><td>+</td><td>$.50</td><td>=</td><td>$2.50</td></tr>
<tr><td>one dollar</td><td></td><td>two dollars</td><td></td><td>two dollars and fifty cents</td><td></td><td></td></tr>
</table>

```
  $1.00
   1.00
+   .50
------
  $2.50
```

<table>
<tr><td>$.50</td><td>+</td><td>$.50</td><td>+</td><td>$.05</td><td>=</td><td>$1.05</td></tr>
<tr><td>fifty cents</td><td></td><td>one dollar</td><td></td><td>one dollar and five cents</td><td></td><td></td></tr>
</table>

```
  $ .50
    .50
+   .05
------
  $1.05
```

Count each of these groups of coins and bills from left to
right. As you count, say the words. Then write the sum
in the blanks, using the dollar sign and a decimal point.

1. = $ 1.11

2. = $___.___

3. = $___.___

4. = $___.___

5. = $___.___

6. = $___.___

NAME _____

Write in the blanks the total value of the money in each row on the left. Use the dollar sign and a decimal point.

1.

are worth $2.05

2.

are worth _____

3.

are worth _____

4.

are worth _____

5.

are worth _____

6.

are worth _____

7.    are worth _____

8.    are worth _____

9.   are worth _____

10.  are worth _____

11.  are worth _____

12.  are worth _____

NAME _____

Write in the blanks the total value of the money on the left. Use the dollar sign and a decimal point.

1.

$ 1.27
_____

2.

_____

3.

_____

4.

_____

5.

_____

6.

_____

7.

_____

8.

_____

9.

_____

10.

_____

How Much Is It?

In these exercises, the money has already been counted. If the sum given is correct, write *Yes* in the blank on the right. If the sum is not correct, write *No* in the blank.

1. 5 nickels equal a quarter.   _Yes_

2. 4 nickels and 4 pennies = 1 quarter. _____

3. Three dimes and one quarter equal a half-dollar. _____

4. 30¢ and 40¢ equal 75¢. _____

5. One half-dollar and five dimes = one dollar. _____

6. 5 dimes and 2 quarters equal one dollar. _____

7. $.05 and $.20 equal $.30. _____

8. 6 dimes, 3 nickels, and 1 quarter = 1 dollar. _____

9. 5 half-dollars, 1 quarter, and 5 dimes = $1.75. _____

10. 1 quarter and 5 dimes equal 75¢. _____

11. Two dimes, three nickels, and 25¢ = sixty cents. _____

12. Three nickels and 4 dimes equal fifty cents. _____

13. One half-dollar and $1.25 = $2.75. _____

14. 2 quarters and 10 dimes equal $1.50. _____

15. $.09, 4 dimes, 25¢, and one nickel = 89¢. _____

16. Two dollars, one dime, and 5¢ = $2.15. _____

17. $1.00 and 3 half-dollars = $4. _____

18. One dollar, 3 nickels, and $.08 equal $1.23. _____

19. $3.00, 8 dimes, and a nickel = $3.95. _____

20. 7 quarters, 25¢, and a penny = two dollars and one cent. _____

Add each group of two coins connected by lines. Write the **sums** in the smaller circles. Then add the sums of all of the smaller circles until you get the total value of the money wheel. Write the **total** in the center circle.

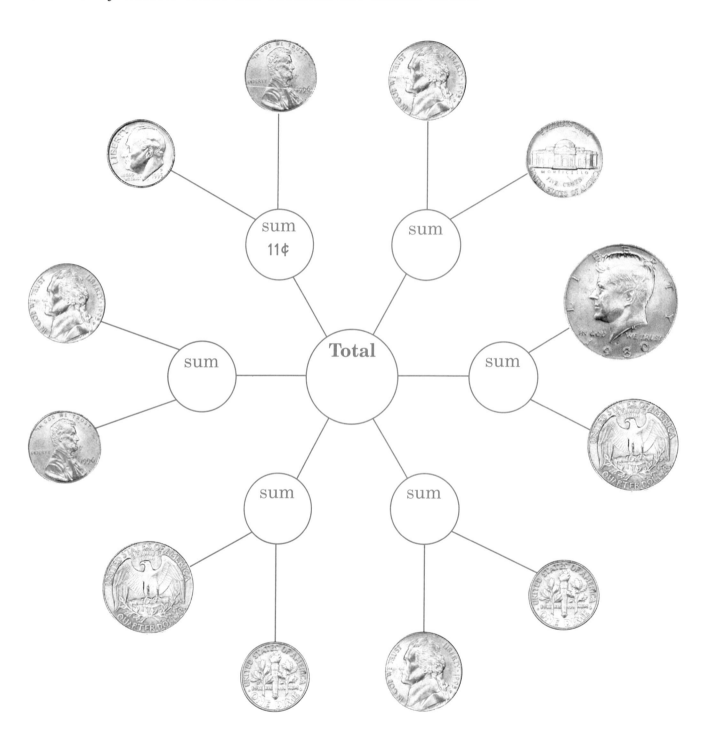

NAME _____

Find the sum of each group of money.

You read: 1 dollar,   1 dime,   1 nickel,   and 2 pennies

You think:

You count: $1 $1.10 $1.15 $1.17

1. 1 dollar, 1 quarter, and 2 dimes   = $ 1.45

2. 2 dollars, 2 quarters, 1 nickel, and 3 pennies   = $___.___

3. 1 dollar, 3 nickels, and 2 pennies   = $___.___

4. 1 dollar, 1 half-dollar, 1 quarter, and 1 penny   = $___.___

5. 3 dollars, 3 dimes, and 1 penny   = $___.___

6. 2 dollars, 3 quarters, and 3 nickels   = $___.___

7. 4 quarters, 2 dimes, 2 nickels, and 3 pennies   = $___.___

8. 1 dollar, 4 dimes, and 3 nickels   = $___.___

9. 4 dollars, 5 dimes, and 5 pennies   = $___.___

10. 1 dollar, 2 quarters, 3 dimes, and 4 pennies   = $___.___

11. 1 dollar, 1 dime, 3 nickels, and 1 penny   = $___.___

12. 2 dollars, 1 half-dollar, and 4 nickels   = $___.___

13. 3 dollars, 1 quarter, and 4 dimes   = $___.___

14. 1 dollar, 2 dimes, 4 nickels, and 8 pennies   = $___.___

15. 4 dollars, 1 quarter, 3 dimes, 1 nickel, and 1 penny   = $___.___

Find the sum of each group of money.

You read:	1 dollar,	2 half-dollars,	and 1 dime
You think:			
You count:	$1	$2	$2.10

16. 1 dollar, 2 half-dollars, and 1 quarter   = $ _2.25_

17. 2 dollars, 3 quarters, 1 nickel, and 2 pennies   = $__·____

18. 1 dollar, 4 quarters, 2 dimes, and 5 pennies   = $__·____

19. 1 dollar, 1 half-dollar, and 3 nickels   = $__·____

20. 3 dollars, 2 quarters, 1 dime, and 2 nickels   = $__·____

21. 2 dollars, 6 dimes, and 4 pennies   = $__·____

22. 2 dollars, 5 nickels, and 7 pennies   = $__·____

23. 4 dollars, 4 dimes, and 4 pennies   = $__·____

24. 1 dollar, 1 dime, 3 nickels, and 3 pennies   = $__·____

25. 2 dollars, 2 quarters, 2 dimes, and 5 pennies   = $__·____

26. 1 dollar, 2 half-dollars, 1 quarter, and 1 dime   = $__·____

27. 3 dollars, 4 dimes, 5 nickels, and 1 penny   = $__·____

28. 3 half-dollars, 1 nickel, and 2 pennies   = $__·____

29. 2 dollars, 5 nickels, and 3 pennies   = $__·____

30. 5 quarters, 2 dimes, and 1 nickel   = $__·____

Fill in the blanks on the right with the number of coins needed to make the amount on the left. There may be more than one correct answer. You only need to find one answer.

1. 1 dime   = __10__ pennies

2. 1 nickel   = _____ pennies

3. 12¢   = _____ dime and _____ pennies

4. 1 dime   = _____ nickels

5. 7¢   = _____ nickel and _____ pennies

6. 18¢   = _____ dime, _____ nickel, and _____ pennies

7. 26¢   = _____ dimes, _____ nickel, and _____ penny

8. 19¢   = _____ dime, _____ nickel, and _____ pennies

9. 25¢   = _____ dimes and _____ nickel

10. 1 quarter   = _____ dime, _____ nickel, and _____ pennies

11. 35¢   = _____ quarter and _____ dime

12. 43¢   = _____ quarter, _____ dime, _____ nickel, and _____ pennies

13. 50¢   = _____ half-dollar

14. 1 half-dollar = _____ pennies

15. 50¢   = _____ nickels

16. 1 half-dollar = _____ quarters

17. 60¢   = _____ half-dollar and _____ dime

18. 66¢   = _____ half-dollar, _____ dime, _____ nickel, and _____ penny

19. 73¢   = _____ half-dollar, _____ dimes, and _____ pennies

20. 65¢   = _____ quarters and _____ nickels

Fill in the blanks on the right with the number of
coins or bills needed to make the amount on the left.

21. 75¢   = __3__ quarters

22. 85¢   = ____ half-dollar, ____ quarter, and ____ nickels

23. 95¢   = ____ half-dollar, ____ quarter, and ____ dimes

24. one dollar = ____ pennies

25. $1.00   = ____ nickels

26. one dollar = ____ dimes

27. $1   = ____ quarters, ____ dimes, and ____ nickel

28. $1.08   = ____ dollar, ____ nickel, and ____ pennies

29. $1.25   = ____ quarters

30. $1.42   = ____ dollar, ____ dimes, and ____ pennies

31. $1.55   = ____ half-dollars and ____ nickel

32. $1.63   = ____ quarters, ____ dime, and ____ pennies

33. $1.80   = ____ dimes

34. $1.95   = ____ dollar, ____ quarters, and ____ nickels

35. two dollars = ____ pennies

36. $2   = ____ half-dollars

37. $2.45   = ____ dollars, ____ quarter, and ____ dimes

38. $2.84   = ____ dollars, ____ nickels, and ____ pennies

39. $3.07   = ____ dollars, ____ nickel, and ____ pennies

40. $3.90   = ____ dollars, ____ quarters, and ____ pennies

41. $4.55   = ____ dollars, ____ half-dollar, and ____ nickel

42. five dollars = ____ half-dollars

Follow the arrows on each path. Add the coins as you
go. Write the sum on each line. Then write the total
sum of all the coins at the bottom of the page.

Path 1　　**Path 2**

Path 1: 25¢ ___ 35¢ ___ ___ ___ Total

Path 2: ___ ___ ___ ___ ___ ___ ___ Total

Total Sum (Path 1 + Path 2) _____

Add the coins in the circles that overlap. Write the sums in the blanks where the circles overlap. Then add together all the coins on the page. Write this sum at the bottom of the page.

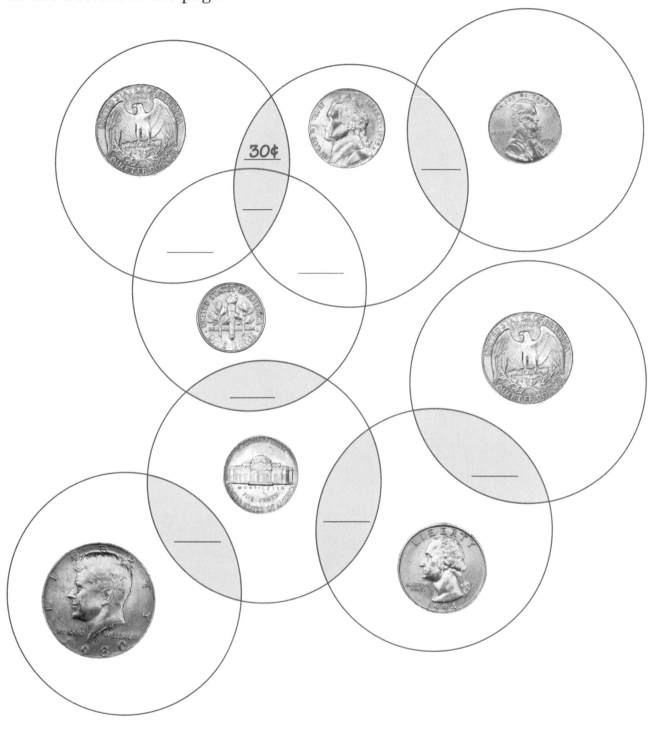

30¢

Total sum of all the coins _____

There are two groups of coins in each of these
exercises. One group is worth more money than the
other group. Make an X under the group worth more
money in each exercise.

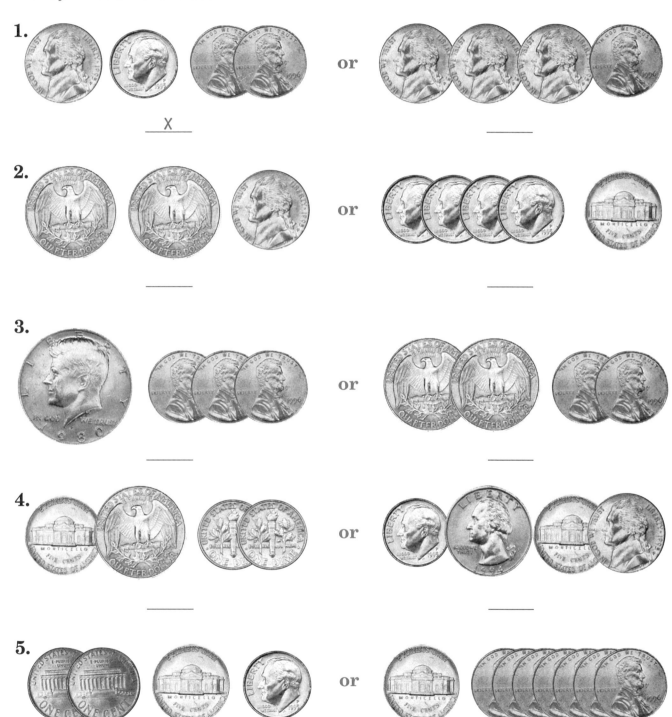

1.   or

      X   _____

2.   or

      _____   _____

3.   or

      _____   _____

4.   or

      _____   _____

5.   or

      _____   _____

6.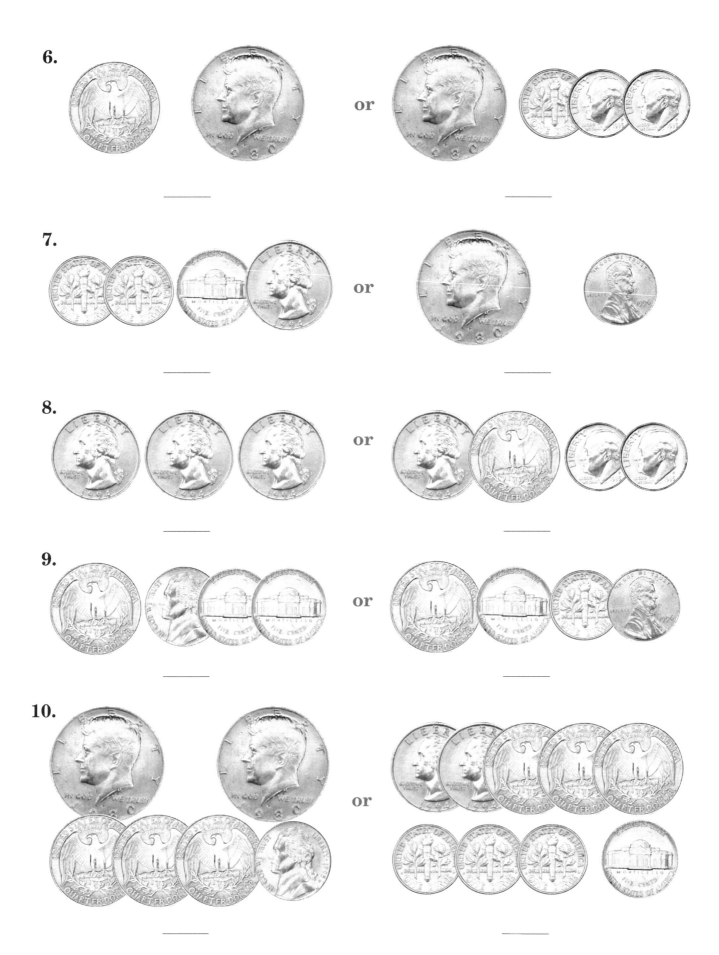

or

_____   _____

7.

or

_____   _____

8.

or

_____   _____

9.

or

_____   _____

10.

or

_____   _____

Which Is Worth More?

There are two different amounts of money in each of these exercises. Make an X in the blank following the amount worth more money in each exercise.

1. 10¢, 25¢, 1¢, 5¢   ——   25¢, 25¢   X̲

2. 5¢, 10¢, 1¢, 1¢   ——   1¢, 1¢, 5¢, 5¢, 1¢   ——

3. 25¢, 50¢, 10¢, 5¢   ——   50¢, 10¢, 10¢, 10¢, 5¢   ——

4. 1¢, 1¢, 1¢, 10¢   ——   5¢, 5¢, 5¢   ——

5. 50¢, 25¢   ——   25¢, 25¢, 10¢, 10¢   ——

6. 25¢, 25¢, 5¢   ——   10¢, 10¢, 10¢, 10¢   ——

7. 5¢, 10¢, 25¢   ——   10¢, 50¢, 1¢   ——

8. $1, 10¢, 5¢, 1¢   —— $1, 5¢, 5¢, 1¢, 1¢   ——

9. 25¢, 50¢, 5¢, 5¢   ——   5¢, 10¢, 25¢, 50¢   ——

10. 50¢, $1, 1¢, 1¢   ——   25¢, 25¢, 1¢, $1   ——

11. 10¢, 10¢, 10¢, 10¢   ——   10¢, 10¢, 5¢, 5¢, 5¢   ——

12. 50¢, 10¢, 5¢, $1   —— $1, 5¢, 10¢, 10¢, 25¢   ——

13. 25¢, 10¢, 25¢, 5¢   ——   10¢, 5¢, 5¢, 5¢, 5¢   ——

14. 25¢, $1, $1, 1¢   ——   10¢, 10¢, $1, $1, 5¢   ——

15. 10¢, 25¢, 50¢, 5¢   ——   25¢, 25¢, 25¢, 10¢   ——

16. 5¢, 5¢, 5¢, 5¢, $1   ——   5¢, $1, 1¢, 10¢, 10¢   ——

17. $1, $1, 10¢, 10¢, 5¢ ——   5¢, 50¢, 50¢, 25¢, $1   ——

18. 5¢, 50¢, 50¢, 50¢   ——   25¢, 25¢, 50¢, 50¢, 10¢   ——

19. 50¢, $1, $1, 1¢   ——   25¢, 25¢, 50¢, 50¢, $1   ——

20. $1, $1, 50¢   ——   5¢, 1¢, $1, $1, $1   ——

Add the coins between the spokes of the wheel. Start with the center coin each time and work out to the rim of the wheel. Write the totals in the blanks along the rim.

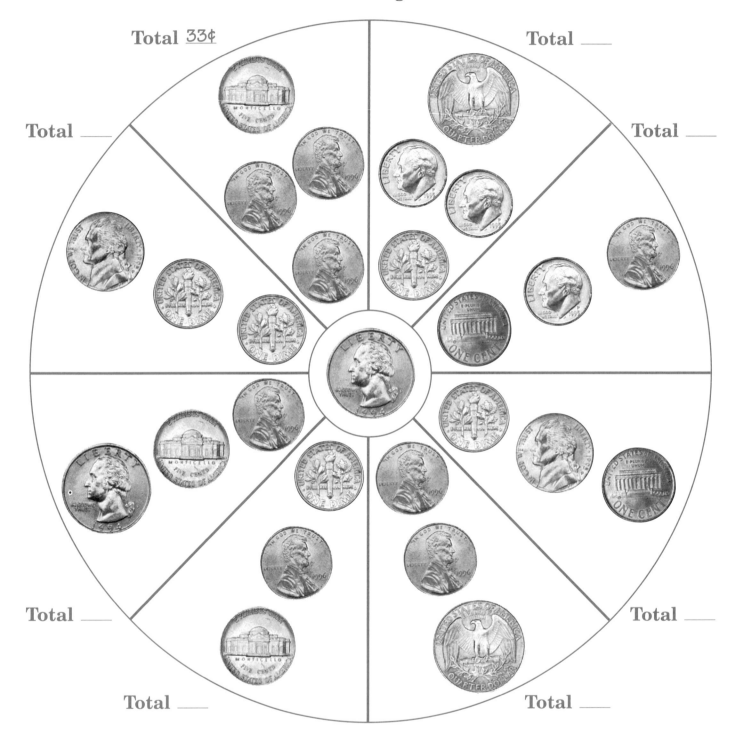

Total 33¢

Total ___

Total ___

Total ___

Total ___

Total ___

Total ___

Total ___

Add the totals around the rim of the wheel. What is the sum? _____

Each of these exercises shows two amounts of money.
If the money on the left is worth more, write *L* in the
blank. If the money on the right is worth more, write *R*
in the blank.

1.

   R

2.

   _____

3.

   _____

4.

   _____

5.

   _____

6.   _____

7.   _____

8.   _____

9.     _____

10.   _____

Draw a line under the larger amount of money in each exercise.

1. <u>8 pennies, 2 dimes</u>   1 quarter, 2 pennies

2. 2 dimes, 5 pennies   1 quarter, 1 dime

3. 6 nickels, 12 pennies   6 dimes, 7 pennies

4. 2 dimes, 5 nickels   2 quarters

5. 1 half-dollar   1 nickel, 4 dimes

6. 7 dimes, 2 pennies   1 half-dollar, 1 dime

7. 4 quarters, 3 nickels   9 dimes, 9 pennies

8. 1 half-dollar, 1 dime   2 quarters, 3 nickels

9. 8 dimes, 2 pennies   3 quarters, 2 nickels

10. 2 half-dollars   3 quarters, 2 dimes

11. 2 dollars, 2 dimes   3 half-dollars, 2 quarters

12. 4 dimes, 3 pennies   6 nickels, 1 dime

13. 1 dollar   4 quarters, 3 dimes

14. 5 quarters, 2 nickels   1 dollar, 6 nickels

15. 8 dimes, 1 quarter   2 half-dollars

Count each line of coins from the center out going up, down, across, and diagonally. Write the totals in the answer boxes. You may use a calculator.

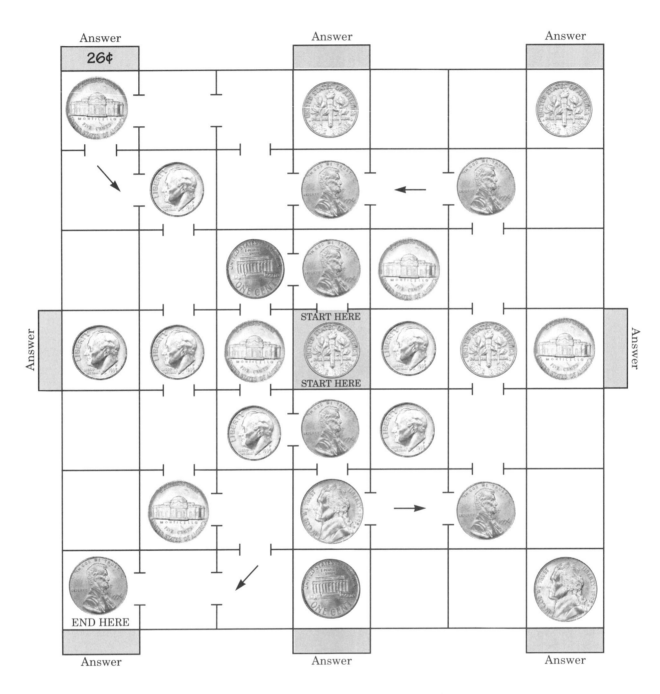

Answer

26¢

Answer

Answer

Answer

START HERE

START HERE

Answer

END HERE

Answer

Answer

Answer

Now, to go through the maze, start in the center and follow the openings through each square. Add each coin as you pass through the maze. Write the total value below.

NAME _____

Arrange the amounts of money in order from the smallest to the largest. Write them in order in the blanks using numbers, the dollar sign, and a decimal point.

1. eight cents, five cents, fourteen cents, twelve cents

   __$ .05__ , __$ .08__ , __$ .12__ , __$ .14__

2. forty-two cents, ten cents, eleven cents, two cents, fifteen cents

   _____ , _____ , _____ , _____ , _____

3. eighteen cents, one cent, eighty cents, thirteen cents, seven cents

   _____ , _____ , _____ , _____ , _____

4. nineteen cents, two cents, forty-one cents, sixty cents, eighteen cents

   _____ , _____ , _____ , _____ , _____

5. one dollar, thirty cents, fourteen cents, two cents, ninety cents

   _____ , _____ , _____ , _____ , _____

6. fifty cents, eighty-eight cents, one cent, one dollar, seventy cents

   _____ , _____ , _____ , _____ , _____

7. three dollars, ten cents, twenty cents, six dollars, four dollars

   _____ , _____ , _____ , _____ , _____

8. eighty-nine cents, two dollars, fifty-one cents, forty-eight cents

   _____ , _____ , _____ , _____

9. one dollar and fifty cents, three dollars and thirty cents, seventy-five cents, two dollars and thirty cents, two dollars

   _____ , _____ , _____ , _____ , _____

10. four dollars and thirty-two cents, two dollars and ten cents, four dollars and seventy-one cents, one dollar and five cents, three dollars

   _____ , _____ , _____ , _____ , _____

Arrange the amounts of money in order from the smallest to the largest. Write them in the blanks, from the top down, using words.

11. 18¢ 3¢ 36¢ 54¢

three cents

eighteen cents

thirty-six cents

fifty-four cents

12. 16¢ 86¢ 92¢ 37¢

_____

_____

_____

_____

13. 11¢ 8¢ 14¢ 3¢ 24¢

_____

_____

_____

_____

14. 30¢ 70¢ 40¢ 90¢ 12¢

_____

_____

_____

_____

15. 19¢ 73¢ 70¢ 74¢ $1.00

_____

_____

_____

16. 44¢ $2 20¢ 22¢ $2.20

_____

_____

_____

Add each group of coins and write your answers next to each group. Arrange these amounts of money in order from the smallest to the largest. Write them in order in the blanks, using numbers. Use the dollar sign and decimal point for amounts over a dollar, and the cents sign for amounts under a dollar.

1. • two dimes and one nickel 25¢
   • three dimes 30¢
   • one quarter and two pennies 27¢
   • one dime and two nickels 20¢

   _20¢_ _25¢_ _27¢_ _30¢_

2. • six dimes
   • six nickels
   • five quarters
   • one half-dollar and two quarters

   _____ _____ _____ _____

3. • four dimes
   • one quarter and two dimes
   • one quarter, one dime, and one penny
   • two dimes and three nickels

   _____ _____ _____ _____

4. • three quarters and two dimes
   • one half-dollar and four dimes
   • two quarters and four nickels
   • three quarters and ten pennies

   _____ _____ _____ _____

5. • two quarters, one dime, and one nickel
   • three quarters
   • one quarter and three dimes
   • one half-dollar

   _____ _____ _____ _____

6. • four quarters and one nickel
   • one half-dollar and three quarters
   • one dollar, one dime, and one nickel
   • one half-dollar and six dimes

   _____ _____ _____ _____

7. • one dime and three nickels
   • nineteen pennies
   • one dime and ten pennies
   • five nickels and one penny

   _____ _____ _____ _____

8. • two half-dollars and three dimes
   • one dollar and two quarters
   • one dollar and four nickels
   • one half-dollar and fifty pennies

   _____ _____ _____ _____

Coin Clusters

Add each group of coins connected by lines. Write the totals in the blanks in the center. Then put the totals in order from the smallest amount to the largest amount. Write these totals at the bottom of the page.

31¢

1. __31¢__   2. _____   3. _____   4. _____   5. _____   6. _____

Which Coin Is Missing?

Write the correct amount on the blank coin to make the
total value of the coins equal to the amount on the right.

1.     **= 64¢**

2.    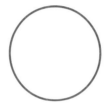 **= $1**

3.    **= 19¢**

4. 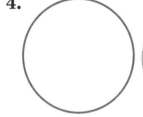     **= 93¢**

5.  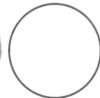   **= 67¢**

6.   **= 40¢**

7.  = 45¢

8. = 71¢

9. = $1.30

10.  = 80¢

11.  = 39¢

12.  = $1.25

Which Coins Are Missing?

Write the correct amounts on the blank coins to make the total value of the coins equal to the amount on the right.

1.  25¢   1¢ 1¢ = 53¢

2.     = 55¢

3.     = 51¢

4. 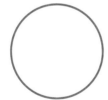   = 46¢

5.  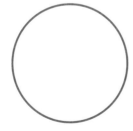 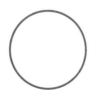   = 82¢

6. 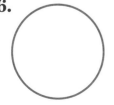     = 81¢

7. ◯ ◯ 　　　=　70¢

8. ◯ ◯　　　=　$1.25

9. ◯ ◯ 　　　=　47¢

10. ◯ ◯ 　　　=　85¢

11. ◯ ◯ 　　　=　$1.60

12. ◯ ◯　　　=　99¢

Write in the blanks the total value of the coins and bills on the left.
Choose your answers from this list. You may use an answer more than once.

ninety-five cents	fifty-five cents	thirty-two cents
sixteen cents	sixty-two cents	two dollars
one dollar	fifty-nine cents	ninety cents

1.

_____ *sixteen cents* _____

2.

_____

3.

_____

4.

_____

5.

_____

6.

_____

7.

_____

8.

_____

9.

_____

10.

_____

NAME _____

Write in the blanks the total value of the coins and bills on the left. Use numbers and a decimal point.

1.

$ .35

2.

$.____

3.

$.____

4.

$.____

5.

$.____

6.

$.____

7.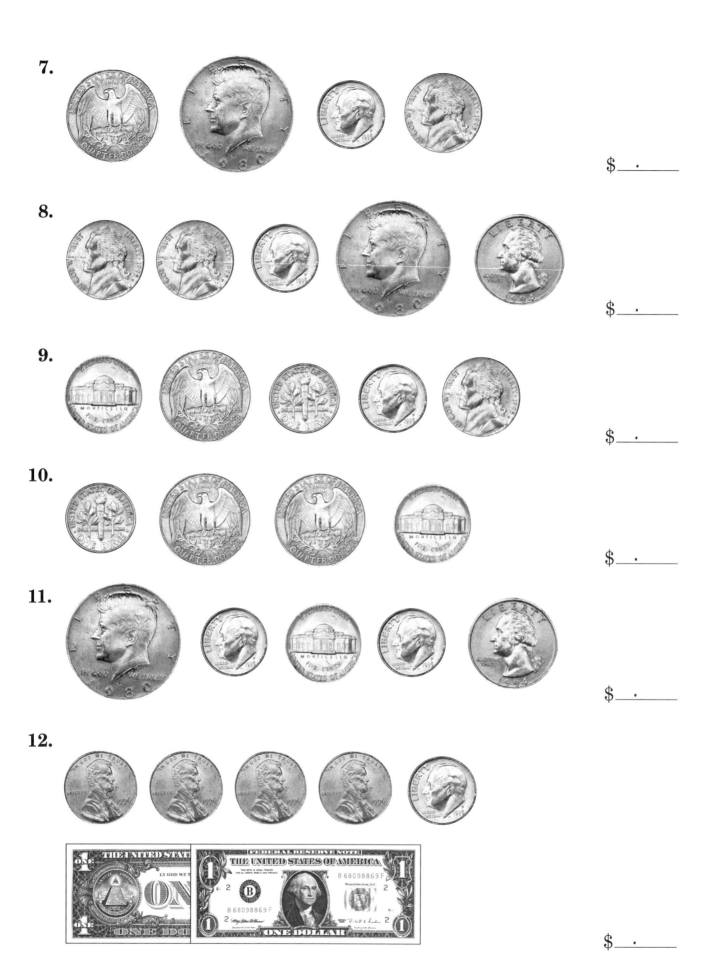

$___.___

8.

$___.___

9.

$___.___

10.

$___.___

11.

$___.___

12.

$___.___

How Much Is It?

Write in the blanks the total value of the coins and
bills on the left. Use numbers.

1.

    $ __3.40__

2.

   $___.___

3.

  $___.___

4.

   $___.___

5.

   $___.___

one hundred three 103

The Money Wheel

Add each group of two money values connected by lines.
Write the **sums** in the smaller circles. Then add the
sums of all of the smaller circles to get the total value of
the money wheel. Write the **total** in the center circle.

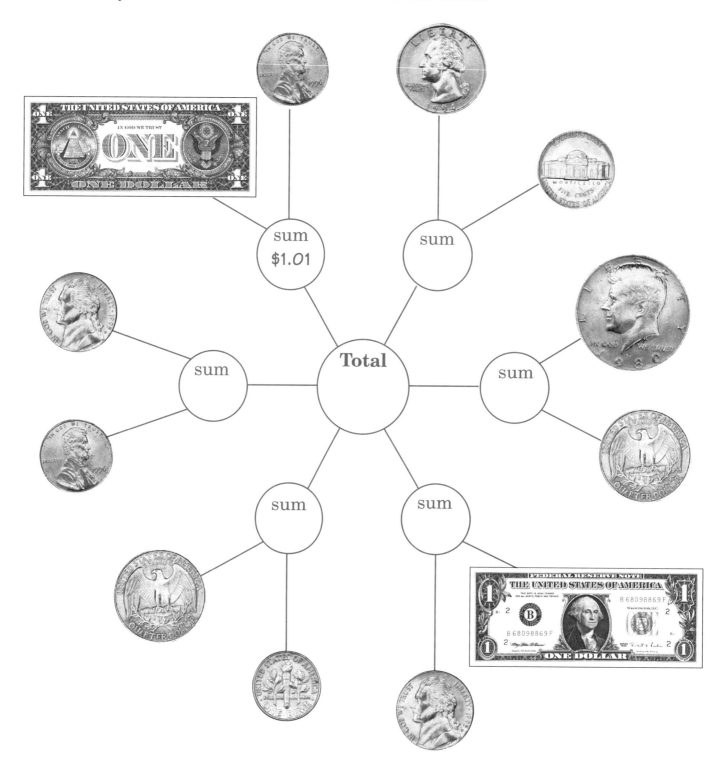

How Much Is It?

Write in the blanks the total value of the money on the left. Use numbers.

1. 5 dollars, 1 quarter, and 2 dimes $= \quad$ $\$\underline{\text{5.45}}$

2. 3 half-dollars, 4 dimes, and 6 pennies $= \quad$ $\$\underline{\quad}.\underline{\quad}$

3. 4 quarters, 8 nickels, and 3 pennies $= \quad$ $\$\underline{\quad}.\underline{\quad}$

4. 20 dimes, 3 quarters, and 3 nickels $= \quad$ $\$\underline{\quad}.\underline{\quad}$

5. 4 dollars, 2 half-dollars, and 1 dime $= \quad$ $\$\underline{\quad}.\underline{\quad}$

6. 8 quarters, 4 nickels, and 15 pennies $= \quad$ $\$\underline{\quad}.\underline{\quad}$

7. 7 dollars, 1 half-dollar, and 1 quarter $= \quad$ $\$\underline{\quad}.\underline{\quad}$

8. 5 quarters, 4 dimes, and 3 nickels $= \quad$ $\$\underline{\quad}.\underline{\quad}$

9. 6 dollars, 1 quarter, and 10 nickels $= \quad$ $\$\underline{\quad}.\underline{\quad}$

10. 4 half-dollars, 2 dimes, and 2 nickels $= \quad$ $\$\underline{\quad}.\underline{\quad}$

11. 8 dollars, 2 half-dollars, and 9 pennies $= \quad$ $\$\underline{\quad}.\underline{\quad}$

12. 5 dollars, 4 half-dollars, and 7 nickels $= \quad$ $\$\underline{\quad}.\underline{\quad}$

13. 30 dimes, 20 nickels, and 13 pennies $= \quad$ $\$\underline{\quad}.\underline{\quad}$

14. 6 dollars, 2 quarters, 1 nickel, and 1 penny $= \quad$ $\$\underline{\quad}.\underline{\quad}$

15. 8 half-dollars, 3 dimes, and 6 nickels $= \quad$ $\$\underline{\quad}.\underline{\quad}$

16. 7 quarters, 1 half-dollar, and 7 pennies $= \quad$ $\$\underline{\quad}.\underline{\quad}$

17. 5 half-dollars, 1 dime, 1 nickel, and 8 pennies $= \quad$ $\$\underline{\quad}.\underline{\quad}$

18. 7 dollars, 5 quarters, and 5 nickels $= \quad$ $\$\underline{\quad}.\underline{\quad}$

19. 3 dollars, 4 half-dollars, 4 quarters, and 10 dimes $= \quad$ $\$\underline{\quad}.\underline{\quad}$

20. 9 dollars, 3 quarters, 2 dimes, and 4 pennies $= \quad$ $\$\underline{\quad}.\underline{\quad}$

21. 2 dollars, 3 quarters, and 1 dime = $ _2.85_

22. 1 dollar, 4 dimes, and 3 nickels = $__.___

23. 6 dollars and 5 quarters = $__.___

24. 1 dollar, 3 half-dollars, and 3 nickels = $__.___

25. 2 half-dollars, 3 quarters, and 15 pennies = $__.___

26. 4 dollars, 4 quarters, and 4 dimes = $__.___

27. 10 dimes, 4 nickels, and 7 pennies = $__.___

28. 7 dollars, 3 quarters, and 3 dimes = $__.___

29. 9 dollars, 6 nickels, and 4 pennies = $__.___

30. 11 dimes, 2 nickels, and 6 pennies = $__.___

31. 5 quarters, 4 dimes, and 2 nickels = $__.___

32. 3 dollars, 2 half-dollars, and 4 quarters = $__.___

33. 2 dollars, 6 quarters, and 6 dimes = $__.___

34. 8 dollars, 1 half-dollar, and 3 quarters = $__.___

35. 3 half-dollars, 4 dimes, and 4 nickels = $__.___

36. 8 dollars, 2 quarters, and 3 dimes = $__.___

37. 6 quarters, 3 dimes, and 3 nickels = $__.___

38. 5 dollars, 5 quarters, and 1 nickel = $__.___

39. 3 dollars, 3 quarters, and 4 dimes = $__.___

40. 7 dollars, 3 quarters, and 2 pennies = $__.___

How Many Are There?

Fill in the blanks on the right with the number of
coins or bills needed to make the amount on the left.
There may be more than one correct answer. You only
need to find one answer.

1. $2.15   =   __2__ dollars, __1__ dime, and __5__ pennies

2. $3.76   =   _____ dollars, _____ quarters, and _____ penny

3. $3.50   =   _____ half-dollars

4. $6.35   =   _____ dollars and _____ nickels

5. $5.83   =   _____ dollars, _____ dimes, and _____ pennies

6. $2.25   =   _____ quarters

7. $1.10   =   _____ dimes

8. $7.48   =   _____ dollars, _____ dimes, and _____ pennies

9. $4.56   =   _____ dollars, _____ half-dollar, and _____ pennies

10. $8.95   =   _____ dollars, _____ quarters, and _____ nickels

11. $5.07   =   _____ dollars, _____ nickel, and _____ pennies

12. $ .82   =   _____ quarters and _____ pennies

13. $1.59   =   _____ dimes, _____ nickel, and _____ pennies

14. $6.22   =   _____ dollars, _____ nickels, and _____ pennies

15. $9.70   =   _____ dollars, _____ quarters, and _____ dimes

16. $4.35   =   _____ half-dollars and _____ nickels

17. $7.45   =   _____ dollars, _____ quarter, and _____ dimes

18. $3.33   =   _____ dollars, _____ dimes, and _____ pennies

19. $8.85   =   _____ dollars, _____ quarters, and _____ nickels

20. $9.19   =   _____ dollars, _____ nickels, and _____ pennies

21. $1.85 = __1__ dollar, __3__ quarters, and __1__ dime

22. $2.22 = _____ dollars, _____ dimes, and _____ pennies

23. $5.25 = _____ dollars and _____ nickels

24. $4.27 = _____ dollars, _____ quarter, and _____ pennies

25. $2.00 = _____ quarters

26. $5.56 = _____ dollars, _____ quarters, and _____ pennies

27. $1.30 = _____ quarters and _____ nickel

28. $7.29 = _____ dollars, _____ nickels, and _____ pennies

29. $ .95 = _____ half-dollar, _____ quarter, and _____ dimes

30. $6.33 = _____ dollars, _____ dimes, and _____ pennies

31. $2.10 = _____ quarters and _____ dime

32. $6.97 = _____ dollars, _____ dimes, and _____ pennies

33. $4.65 = _____ dollars, _____ quarters, and _____ nickels

34. $1.80 = _____ half-dollars, _____ quarters, and _____ dimes

35. $3.70 = _____ dollars, _____ quarters, and _____ nickels

36. $ .80 = _____ quarters and _____ dimes

37. $8.17 = _____ dollars, _____ dime, and _____ pennies

38. $7.31 = _____ dollars, _____ dimes, and _____ penny

39. $2.25 = _____ dollar, _____ half-dollars, and _____ quarter

40. $7.77 = _____ dollars, _____ dimes, and _____ pennies

Here are some questions about coins. Think about each question before you write your answer in the blank. There may be more than one correct answer. How many can you find?

1. What 4 coins equal one dollar? _____ 4 quarters _____

2. What 5 coins equal a quarter? _____

3. What 3 coins equal 25¢? _____

4. What 6 coins equal thirty cents? _____

5. What 7 coins equal 45¢? _____

6. What 5 coins equal eighty-five cents? _____

   _____

7. What 7 coins equal 75¢? _____

   _____

8. What 3 coins equal $1.00? _____

   _____

9. What 8 coins equal $1.05? _____

   _____

10. What 6 coins equal $1.22? _____

    _____

11. What 8 coins equal 75¢? _____

_____

12. What 9 coins equal 87¢? _____

_____

13. What 8 coins equal $2.25? _____

_____

14. What 8 coins equal $2.50? _____

_____

15. What 7 coins equal 90¢? _____

_____

16. What 10 coins equal $1.82? _____

_____

17. What 8 coins equal $1.56? _____

_____

18. What 9 coins equal $2.25? _____

_____

19. What 9 coins equal $1.06? _____

_____

20. What 8 coins equal 99¢? _____

_____

21. What bill and coin equal $1.50? _____

_____

22. What bill and 5 coins equal $2.25? _____

_____

When you make a call on a pay telephone, you use coins. The coins you use are the quarter, the dime, and the nickel. The telephone operator will tell you how much money to deposit. Follow the telephone operator's instructions in each of these problems. Make X's under the coins you must deposit for your call.

1. On your call to Tampa, deposit 55¢, please.

   X   _____   X   X   _____   _____

2. On your call to San Francisco, deposit 25¢, please.

_____   _____   _____   _____   _____   _____

3. On your call to El Paso, deposit 85¢, please.

_____   _____   _____   _____   _____   _____

4. On your call to Mobile, deposit $1.15, please.

_____   _____   _____   _____   _____   _____

5. On your call to New York, deposit 95¢, please.

_____   _____   _____   _____   _____   _____   _____

6. On your call to Baltimore, deposit 40¢, please.

_____   _____   _____   _____   _____   _____

7. On your call to Philadelphia, deposit 80¢, please.

_____   _____   _____   _____   _____   _____   _____

8. On your call to Denver, deposit $1.00, please.

_____ _____ _____ _____ _____ _____ _____ _____

9. On your call to Chicago, deposit 90¢, please.

_____ _____ _____ _____ _____ _____ _____ _____

10. On your call to Los Angeles, deposit 65¢, please.

_____   _____   _____   _____   _____   _____   _____

NAME _____

These items are found in a grocery store.

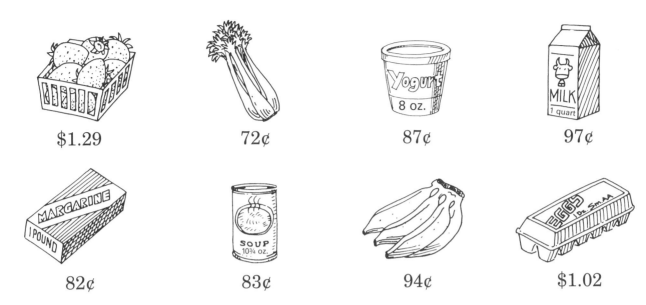

$1.29   72¢   87¢   97¢

82¢   83¢   94¢ $1.02

Show that you know how to use coins. Make an X under
the item that costs as much as the coins on the left.

1.

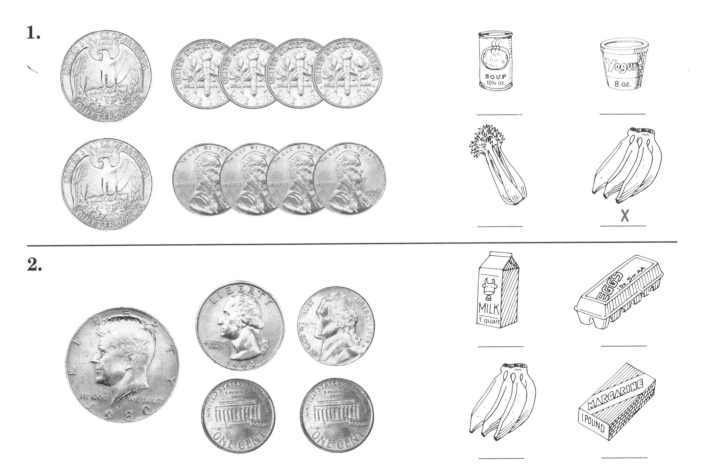

2.

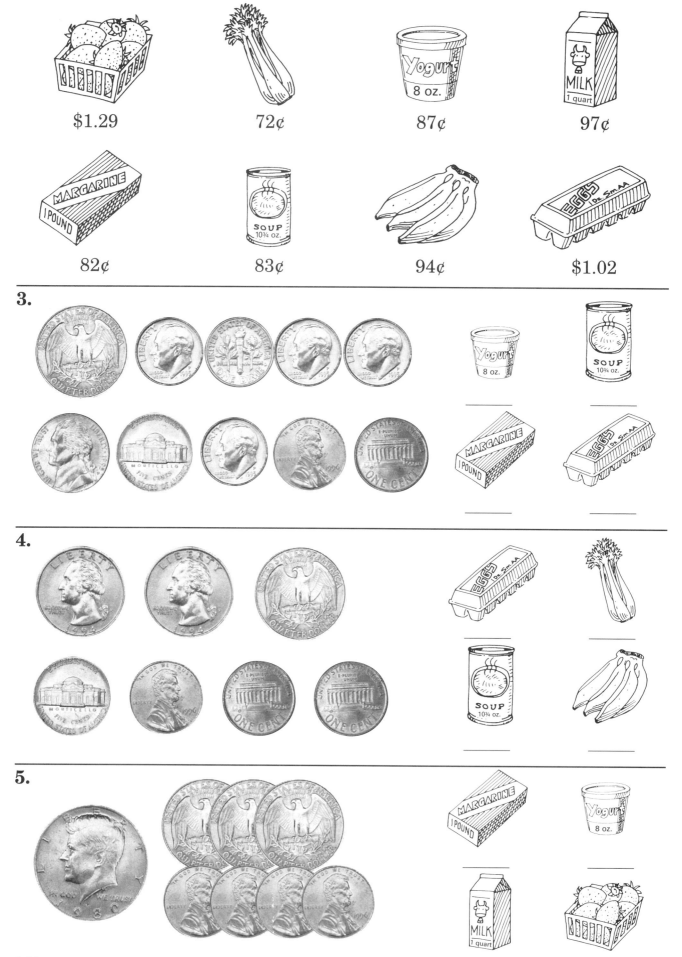

$1.29   72¢   87¢   97¢

82¢   83¢   94¢ $1.02

3.

4.

5.

These items are found in a drugstore.

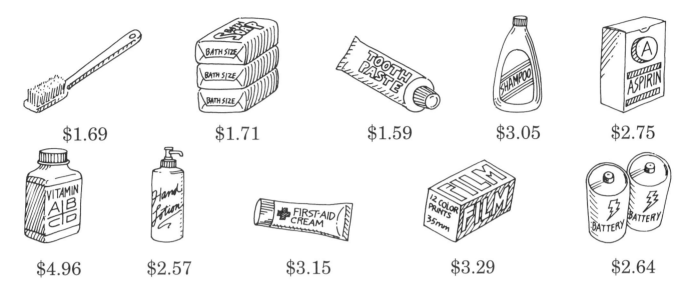

$1.69 $1.71 $1.59 $3.05 $2.75

$4.96 $2.57 $3.15 $3.29 $2.64

Show that you know how to use money. Make an X under the item that costs as much as the coins and bills on the left.

$1.69 $1.71 $1.59 $3.05 $2.75

$4.96 $2.57 $3.15 $3.29 $2.64

3.

_____   _____

_____   _____

4.

_____   _____

_____   _____

5.

_____   _____

_____   _____

When we want to buy something that costs more than four or five dollars, it is difficult to carry around that much money in coins. It can also be confusing to carry around a lot of dollar bills. Let's take a look at some of the other bills that we use most often, and see how much each is worth.

$5.00

Abraham Lincoln's picture is on the front.

The back shows the Lincoln Memorial in Washington, D.C.

 +  +  +  + =

$10.00

Alexander Hamilton's picture is on the front.

The back shows the Treasury Building in Washington, D.C.

 +  =

$20.00

Andrew Jackson's picture is on the front.

The back shows the White House in Washington, D.C.

Write the totals of the following bills in the blanks.
It is easier to count the larger bills first.

1.
= $ _____13.00_____

2.
= $ _____

3.

= $ _____

4.
= $ _____

5.
= $ _____

6.
= $ _____

Shopping Quiz

These items are found in a sporting goods store.

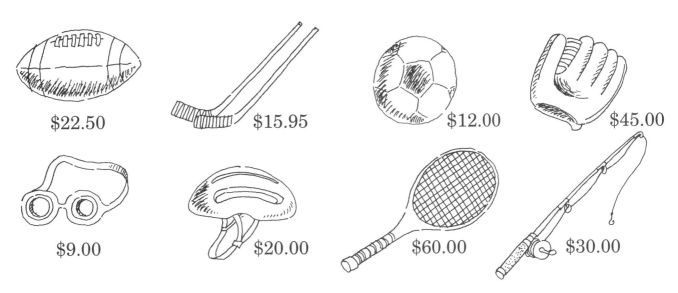

$22.50 $15.95 $12.00 $45.00

$9.00 $20.00 $60.00 $30.00

Show that you know how to use money. Make an X under the item that costs as much as the coins and bills on the left.

 1.

_____   _____

_____   X

 2.

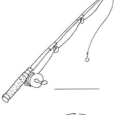

_____   _____

_____   _____

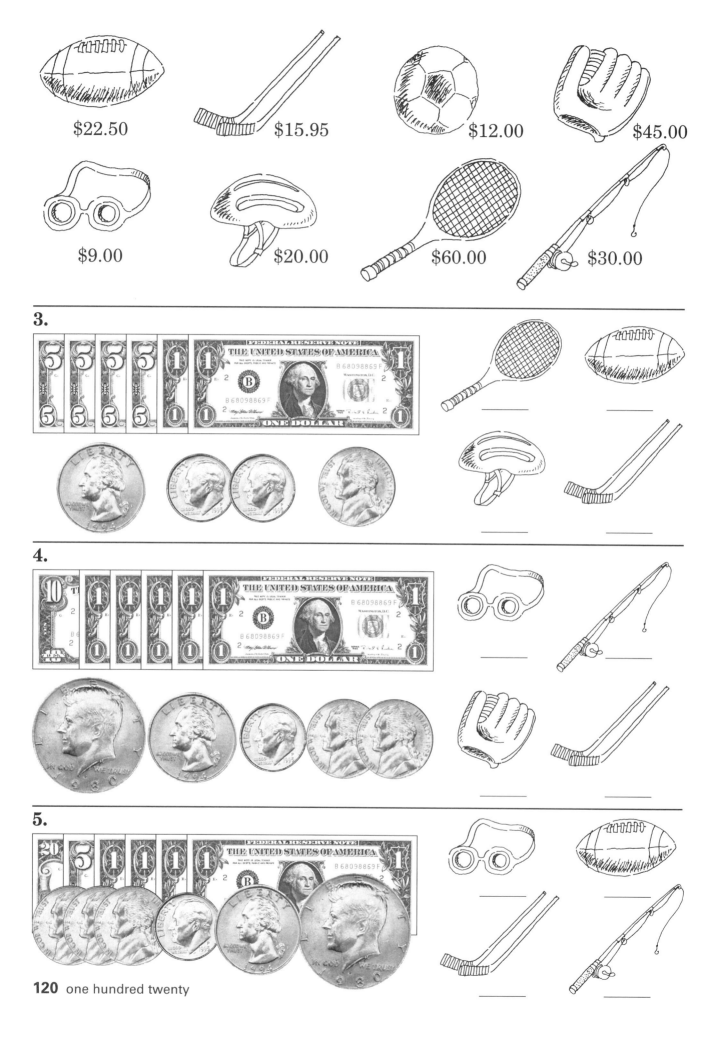

$22.50 $15.95 $12.00 $45.00

$9.00 $20.00 $60.00 $30.00

3.

4.

5.

NAME _____

These items are found in a clothing store.

$15.00 $24.95 $10.00 $30.00

$29.99 $22.00 $18.00 $17.00

Show that you know how to use money. Make an X under the item that costs as much as the coins and bills on the left.

1.

_____   X

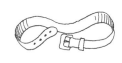

_____   _____

2.

_____   _____

_____   _____

$15.00

$24.95

$10.00

$30.00

$29.99

$22.00

$18.00

$17.00

3.

4.

5.

Shopping Quiz

The items at the right are found in a bookstore. Make X's
under the coins and bills you would use to pay for these items.

1.

X   X   X   X   ___   ___   ___   X

___   X   ___   X   ___   X   ___   ___

$9.60

2.

$2.25

3.

$3.45

4.

_____

$9.40

_____

5.

_____

$4.65

_____

6.

_____

$15.55

_____

Posttest 1

In these exercises, you are buying different things in a store. Make an X under each item that costs as much as the money below the items.

1.

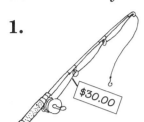 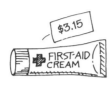  

$30.00 $3.15 $9.00 $3.45

_____ _____ _____ X _____

2.

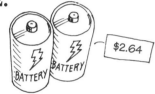   

$2.64 $45.00 $9.40 $2.75

_____ _____ _____ _____

3.

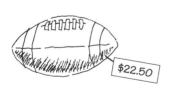   

$22.50 $2.57 $12.00 $9.60

_____ _____ _____ _____

4.

 $1.29    $15.00    $9.00    $1.69

_____   _____   _____   _____

5.

 $22.00    $15.55    $24.95    $17.00

_____   _____   _____   _____

6.

 $4.65    $4.96    $.97    $3.15

_____   _____   _____   _____

NAME _____

In these exercises, you are buying different things in a store. Make X's under the coins and bills you will use to pay for what you buy.

1. You are buying $15.55

You pay with

  X   X   X   X

2. You are buying  $1.02

You pay with

_____ _____ _____ _____ _____ _____ _____ _____

3. You are buying $3.29

You pay with

_____ _____ _____ _____ _____ _____ _____ _____

_____ _____ _____ _____ _____

4. You are buying $4.96

You pay with

___ ___ ___ ___ ___ ___ ___

___ ___ ___

5. You are buying $.97

You pay with

___ ___ ___ ___ ___ ___ ___

6. You are buying $15.00

You pay with

___ ___ ___ ___ ___

___ ___ ___ ___ ___ ___ ___